conquering the
Coast
to
Coast

Kelly Barber

HAZARD PRESS
publishers

Published by Hazard Press Ltd
PO Box 2151
Christchurch
New Zealand
www.hazardpress.co.nz

ISBN 1-877393-17-7

Cover design by Working Ideas

Printed in New Zealand

Contents

Author's note   4

Foreword by Mike Ward   5

Acknowledgements   7

1   A Reawakening   9

2   The Journey Begins   14

3   Fear and Loathing   24

4   Learning to Kayak   32

5   It's All About the Bike   41

6   Matters of the Sole   48

7   Bringing It All Together   52

8   Race Day   59

9   Life on the Road   70

10   Running on Empty   81

11   Bouncing Back   88

12   Doreen Creek to Goat Pass   96

13   Mind Games   108

14   Suffering   118

15   Klondyke   128

16   Crash   134

17   River Antics   142

18   Water Worries   152

19   The Gorge   159

20   The Last Ride   176

Epilogue   198

Author's note

This is more than a story about a man doing the Coast to Coast, New Zealand's premier multi-sport event, one time. I have now actually done the race eight times. However, I have told my story as though it were a single journey and although the vast majority of the story comes from my first race, not all of the specific incidents and events in this book took place during that particular event. My stories are presented as a pastiche, and I make no apology for this slight use of artistic license. Of course the actions and appearance of some characters have been altered slightly to protect the innocent.

Foreword

by Mike Ward

Just prior to the 2006 Coast to Coast race, Kelly Barber's *Conquering the Coast to Coast* manuscript arrived in the post – too late to make a difference to my 24th consecutive display of Coast to Coast mediocrity, but soon enough to highlight the fact that my vast experience isn't about to compensate for my grossly inadequate preparation and nutrition, my sloppy transitions, a total lack of technique and a collection of antique equipment.

Although in 2002 I remained consistent in regard to all of the above behaviours, I eventually got a medal for my 20th Coast to Coast – in spite of not figuring in the results beyond a DNF (Did Not Finish) for the Mountain Run. I did finish but I was disqualified for missing the 2.15 pm cut-off at Klondyke by a trifling 15 minutes. I decided to complete the race anyway. When my crew went to pick up my boat from Mt White Bridge, there were six kayakers waiting for me to arrive and my crew were instructed to get my arse into the river. The cut-off at Woodstock is 7 pm, I paddled in at 8 o'clock and was disqualified again. Not getting to Sumner still wasn't an option, so I started running down to Gorge Bridge. By the time my crew met me with my bike it was well after nine and it was close to one in the morning when I cycled into Sumner. I doubt anyone ever took longer.

There were no crowds, no medal, no Speight's, just my crew, my family, one other competitor and a grumpy Robin Judkins. My medal and beer arrived in the post, courtesy of Kelly Barber, a couple of weeks after the event. He had given me his own.

Kelly's book has shown me the error of my ways. I now know where I have been going wrong. Next year I promise to train, I will oil my chain, my crew will practise the transitions, I will eat, I will learn to roll and I will hydrate. But the real message in this book is that just about anybody prepared to put in the effort could do the Coast to Coast. In an increasingly sedentary world, where adventures are more likely to be experienced secondhand via television or cinema, there is no substitute for the real thing.

So read on, and whether your adventure be a truly gruelling Judkins junket or a local fun-run, go forth and do it. Your friends are likely to be impressed, you will feel healthier (eventually), and I suspect that, like Kelly Barber, you just may 'want to do more with your life, and become a better person'. Certainly life is about to get more interesting.

Acknowledgements

I would like to record my thanks to the people who have helped and supported me during my involvement in the Coast to Coast and the writing of this book:

Dr Paul Petersen for planting the idea. Hugh, Berneen and Sandy, workmates who encouraged my early attempts to train. Don and Margaret Dawson, for their friendship, advice, equipment and many cups of tea. My good friends and faithful support crew Chris Middlemiss, Graham Alexander, Tony Borkus, Andrew Turpin, Mark Elliott and my eldest son Zac. Thanks also to the many people I have trained and raced with over the years: good people with generous natures and adventure in their hearts – Sharon Prutton, Chris Middlemiss, Mike Ward, Morgan Strong, and my brothers Guy, Josh, Jaimie and Matt. And to the great man himself: Robin Judkins (Juddy) for opening doors and making it all possible.

Michael Jacques, who gave me my first opportunity to write about multisport and who is about the best friend you could have in this sport. William Michael of www.windeaters.co.nz who taught me a great deal about writing and did some sterling work tidying up the early manuscript. Mike Bradstock of Bradstock and Associates for his advice and help and for sending me to Hazard Press. Antoinette Wilson, Fiona Gartland and Elizabeth Woods at Hazard Press, who under the guiding genius of Quentin Wilson turn dreams into reality. Thanks especially to Paul Farrow at Paul's Camera Shop, Michael Jacques, Mark Elliott and Don Dawson for the wonderful photos that grace the text.

And last but not least, thanks to my wife and best friend Melissa, for many years of support, advice and for picking me up off the floor for one reason or another. None of this would have been possible without you.

That, as they say, will about do it.

To my parents Nick and Rosalie

Chapter 1

A Reawakening

When I was a child I loved adventure. From as early as I can remember I sought it out. At every opportunity I would gather together like-minded friends, and adventure we would pursue. We went camping, hiking, fishing, swimming and biking. At night we would wear masks to cover our faces and sneak around the neighbourhood for the pure pleasure of it. Sometimes we got caught but we were kids and no one seemed to mind too much. It was a grand time.

But as I grew so did my responsibilities. I did less and less camping, hiking, fishing, swimming and biking and I knew that now there would be a hell of a lot more explaining to do if I got caught with a mask on in someone else's backyard.

Eventually I stopped partaking in real adventures and turned to reading about them. I particularly liked books on tramping and mountaineering – reading about vertical ice walls and the brave fools that climb them excited me and allowed me to lose myself in a world of adventure that reminded me of my childhood.

Reading about adventure had its advantages. For a start, it was safer. I could be deeply engrossed in clinging to a vertical ice wall hundreds of metres above some bottomless chasm, then simply walk off and have a cup of tea. Perils could be 'experienced' from a casual and dispassionate distance, away from the heart-stopping and sphincter-clenching horror of the reality.

But reading about adventure instead of experiencing it had disadvantages. I put on a little weight. Not a huge amount but enough so that at family gatherings my brothers would make fun of me – getting away with it as only family can. I had let myself get too busy for anything other than work and family, but in my heart I still longed for real adventure.

And so it was until one day at the age of 34 I had a conversation that changed my life. It went something like this.

'You're looking very fit, have you just done the Coast to Coast?'

I looked more closely at my friend to check he hadn't had his eyes poked out since we had last met. Nope, they were still there. I couldn't fathom why he thought I was looking fit; and even if I was looking fit why did he think someone of my slothfulness could possibly have participated in an event like the Coast to Coast?

'No, I haven't,' I replied.

'Oh! ... You should do it.'

That was it. Nothing more. It was a few words passed between casual business acquaintances. Over the years I must have had many conversations just like it. Somehow this one was different. I remembered every word and I couldn't stop thinking about it. All day my mind raced over the same thoughts.

Something was awakening inside me and the more I thought about it the more I realised I was developing an unnerving desire for real adventure. I began to feel drunk on the intoxicating thought of this magnificent challenge. The race would not start for eleven months but even if I trained every day it would almost certainly still cause me extreme discomfort.

I had known about the Coast to Coast for a long time but that day for some reason I suddenly wanted to do it. The abruptness of my desire shocked me. It was as if I was a teenager driven by hormones, in love for the first time and coming to the realization that the awkward-looking girl next door was no longer as ugly as an old shoe but had blossomed into a goddess.

Something changed in me that day. By the time I got home from work I knew I was going to do the Coast to Coast.

The Coast to Coast is the granddaddy of all triathlons. Its 243-kilometre course winds across the South Island of New Zealand and takes in some of the most beautiful scenery the world has to offer. It is unique in that it is the only multisport race on the planet that crosses a nation (albeit a smallish one) from west to east in a single day (or two should you prefer to stop at halfway for a night under canvas). It is quite unlike its more conventional urban cousin the Ironman, in which competitors swim, bike and run predominantly within the confines of the city, its beginning and end points decided and changed at the whim of the organiser. The Coast to Coast is different. The adventurers that attempt this race run, bike and kayak their way from the Tasman Sea to the Pacific Ocean through native forest, across mountain streams, over a mountain pass, down raging rapids and churning gorge and finally across a seemingly endless plain.

It is not just a race but also a journey from one coast to another; and therein lies much of its attraction. If it were from coast to Bob's Bar and Grill it might attract a certain following but it's hardly going to capture the public's imagination. Why stop at Bob's Bar and Grill? Why not stop at the next public toilet?

In contrast, the Coast to Coast, by its very name, can begin and end in no other place. It carries with it a sense of completeness. It is man (and in increasing numbers women) passing through an environment of scenic wonder – oftentimes harsh, dangerous and almost impassable.

It is the stuff of legend. And somehow, like hundreds before me, I had been drawn to it.

I was not an especially talented athlete at school but despite my limitations I could do one thing reasonably well in my youth: I could run. Not so much fast as long. For generations back on both sides of my family tree there are runners. I like to imagine that being able to run for a long time at a reasonable speed was once a useful skill. Perhaps in the past my ancestors ran from place to place delivering important messages, perhaps even timely messages that saved entire villages from terrible destruction as my ancestors whizzed in to give the alarm – only marginally ahead of impending doom – then lead everyone to safety.

Well, at the very least my ancestors may have been the forefathers of the modern-day courier.

Actually, in my youth I didn't much enjoy running, but I did enjoy winning. And since for me this didn't require a lot of training, I had an uneasy pact with running. I would do it, and even put in a small amount of training, as long as I could win on occasion. As it happened, I did. Not all the time, but often enough to remain interested. I probably would have continued to do well at running had I not, in my late teens, discovered the two great enemies of the runner: beer and cigarettes. My running slowly ground to a halt.

And here I was, years later, thinking of resurrecting my running career. The lure of the Coast to Coast was compelling. On one level was the significance of crossing my country from one side to the other. Not only seeing the heart of a beautiful country but also being out in it, running over its spine, the Southern Alps, tasting its crisp clear water and feeling the cool damp of the forests. Like many New Zealanders, from an early age I had felt drawn to explore the bush and the mountains and in my teens I spent many days tramping in the hills. Now I was being beckoned back. The pull was strong.

On a more personal level there was the appeal of a great challenge; of feeling the pride of resurrecting my body and making a journey back to health after years of neglect. I hoped I could get back to a good level of fitness, convert some fat to muscle and free myself of the beer and cigarettes that had started out as friends but of late had turned on me.

I also wanted the glory. I wanted to do it because it is hard and everyone knows it. I wanted bragging rights. Here was the sort of thing I could nonchalantly throw into a conversation at a party and draw gasps of admiration. I imagined my witty anecdotes causing raucous laughter as I took my audience on an emotional rollercoaster; they would be hanging on my every word as I, the hardened adventurer, made light of countless perils. In short, I wanted to be the Marlboro man – but without the cigarettes or the horse.

Now that my mind was made up and starting to fill with delusions of grandeur it was time to face reality. First I had to confront what was likely to be the biggest obstacle to achieving my new purpose in life. It was time to ask my wife.

I knew that to get her approval for a project of this size I was going to have to approach the matter with delicacy. On the positive side it had been quite some time since the accidental death of her roses at the hand of my liberal weed-spraying programme. And I had been active in doing my share of the housework. She had recently even commented on how much she appreciated my help with the vacuuming (little knowing how useful the thing is for disposing of Lego and other pesky toys).

I concluded that a bunch of flowers would be just the ticket. I would wing it from there.

She liked the flowers. But her day had been a challenging one filling in for a sick teacher at a local school so I waited until after dinner.

'I've decided...' her look seemed stern so I changed tack. 'Um... I want to do the Coast to Coast. Whaddaya think?'

She continued what she was doing. I could have painted the room in the time it took her to answer.

'You're quite serious?'

'Yep.'

'How long have you been thinking about this?'

'Since this morning.'

I knew where this was heading and started to feel a little foolish.

There was another long silence. I would only have had time to mow the lawn.

'You might need to think this through a bit more.'

'I have, and I really want to do it.'

'Oh, really? How far is it exactly?'

'I don't know.'

'How do you enter?'

'I've no idea.'

Point taken. I began my search for information.

Chapter 2

The Journey Begins

Sitting in his kayak cruising down a river in 1980 a man by the name of Robin Judkins had a moment of clarity and the idea of the Coast to Coast was born. If the idea had occurred to almost anyone else in New Zealand probably it would never have become a reality, but Robin Judkins is no ordinary man.

During the 1970s two hugely important events in his life began to unlock his creative genius. The first was his marriage to Lorraine. This gave rise to the second important event: his confrontation of, and eventual victory over, alcoholism. In a hopelessly downward spiral, Judkins was delivered an ultimatum by his new bride. Lorraine demanded he give up the drink or face losing her. He knew she was deadly serious, and he chose wisely. Having decided that he needed to get out of his current environment the couple packed up and moved from Sydney, Australia, back to their homeland, New Zealand.

Settling in the small South Island town of Wanaka on the edge of the Southern Alps, Judkins, an avid skier, took odd jobs before becoming sole ski patroller at a local ski field. While he loved the freedom and beauty of the mountains Judkins had a job to do and he took it seriously. His responsibility as ski patroller included the enforcement of safety rules. Even though he had never been a great fan of officialdom, bureaucrats or their silly rules, one thing he would not compromise on was the safety of those under his care. So when his concerns over avalanche danger were not taken seriously he resigned (after a trade-mark shouting match with his employer). Days later he was running his own kayaking business with a close mate.

In addition to regular shouting matches with anyone with whom he strongly disagreed, another aspect of Judkins' unique personality, and one reason for his success, is his ability to enthuse others. Especially the media. Never one to miss an opportunity, Judkins convinced a member of the New Zealand House of Representatives to open his new venture, and to kayak the river, and had local newspapers turn up to witness the event. To Judkins it wasn't important whether people thought his venture would succeed or fail, it was just important that they thought about it. And talked about it.

With a developing talent for self-promotion and a vision that extended to renaming his business 'The Outdoor Adventure Centre' Judkins and his business partner and close friend Peter Tocker dreamt up a novel adventure. Their goal was to climb Mt Aspiring and then travel by kayak across a lake and down a couple of rivers to the sea. They called their adventure 'Aspiring to the Pacific', and roped in another friend, experienced mountain guide Paul Scaife, to help with the difficult climb. It was an ambitious plan. Mount Aspiring is New Zealand's eighth-highest peak. Near the top it becomes a three-sided pyramid ending in a perfectly triangular summit. It is no place for the faint-hearted and is considered as difficult to climb as Aoraki Mt Cook, New Zealand's highest peak. (Tragically in 2003 Scaife himself was killed in an avalanche on Aoraki Mt Cook whilst guiding clients. Both of these mountains have seen the loss of many lives, including those of competent climbers.)

Judkins was far from what anyone would call a competent climber. He was in fact entirely afraid of heights. Once, high on the mountain and not roped to his experienced companions, he was so scared he could barely stop shaking. Giving himself a stern talking to, he somehow managed to subdue his fear, regain control, and continue. I guess what I really love about the guy, and what I can most relate to, is what he did upon finally reaching the summit of his own personal Everest. After struggling away on the slopes of Aspiring for hour after hour and finally winning what must have been a desperate battle with his fears, when Judkins reached the summit all he could manage to do was to raise himself to his knees. He was too scared to stand up. Now that is true courage.

When they got down from the mountain the media had latched on to the story and the journey was completed in a blaze of publicity. The power of the media was never lost on Judkins.

He continued to have idea after idea for businesses, races and adventures, and it was only natural that eventually he would combine them successfully. On the way he gained valuable experience in running well-organized, challenging, and above all safe events. By the time he was ready to hold the first Coast to Coast he had become an accomplished 'sports promoter', long before anyone knew what that was.

Having developed the concept of a coast-to-coast race and begun considering how to make it a reality, Judkins decided the best way to ensure he knew what the problems and prospective pitfalls were going to be was to do the course himself. So on 12 December 1982, with a few mates in tow, he set out from Kumara Beach on the west coast of the South Island of New Zealand. Ahead lay a two-day trip across the island that would lay the basis for the race. The party of twelve were mostly friends of Judkins', plus Mark Donovan, a young man from Nelson who had asked to join them because he wanted to practise the course before the first race, which was scheduled for a couple of months later. Donovan even brought his own support crew.

At the beginning of day two those willing to continue had dwindled to seven. As they started down the river Donovan slipped ahead without notifying the others. When his absence was finally noticed Judkins was annoyed. He should have kept with the group. After they had searched for him for some time a trout fisherman on the riverbank told them he'd seen a kayaker go through 90 minutes earlier. Judkins was now angry. When they reached the agreed-upon finish point of the river section, Donovan was nowhere to be seen. The safety-conscious Judkins was now absolutely livid. Donovan had broken a serious rule of the river: never separate from your group.*

Judkins decided to continue but could convince none of the others to accompany him on the last cycle ride to Christchurch and the proposed finish line at Sumner beach. He started alone with only his anger for company. Initially cursing Donovan with every rhythmic stroke of the pedal, he found his anger diminishing the closer he got to his goal. Eventually he reached the beach in the dark and ceremoniously splashed around in the sea, tired but totally satisfied.

Elated to have crossed his country, Judkins knew the course was a

---

* *Mad Dogs: A life on the edge*, Robin Judkins, Hazard Press, Christchurch, 1999.

winner. It had taken him 22 hours and 30 minutes and he had loved every minute of it. But he wasn't the first. The fact remained that on 13 December 1982 Mark Donovan from Nelson became the first person to complete the course. (Ironically, later in the first official Coast to Coast race he would be the only competitor not to finish.)

A few days later Judkins phoned Donovan in Nelson and gave him an earful. 'We searched the river for you. You didn't tell anybody you were going on alone and you didn't even wait for us to get off the river. Why did you do that?' asked Judkins.

'I wanted to finish first,' replied Donovan.

Good answer!

I fumbled my way through the phone book. I was a bit nervous. Finally I found what I was after: 'Judkins'.

This was the person I had to speak to if I was going to find out about the Coast to Coast and I'm not entirely sure why, but I felt a bit intimidated. I suppose it was because I desperately wanted to get into the Coast to Coast and I knew thousands of others did too. I was concerned that if I happened to catch him on a bad day I might annoy him. The competition was not restricted to the race: just getting to the start line was a victory in itself. Over the years the popularity of the event had seen the necessity for Judkins to put together a considerable waiting list of poor fools like myself. The selection process was, apparently, pretty informal and entirely up to him, and he could afford to be choosy – and this was a worry.

Having taken the number and prepared to dial I lost my nerve at the last minute and decided to wait a couple of days until I was feeling a little more confident.

Two days later I dialled and got an answer machine so I hung up. Next day the same thing. Later that day I rang the wrong number twice and the old lady on the end of the phone threatened to call the police if I called again. A couple of days later and I was ready to try again.

It didn't even ring and he was on the line, taking me completely by surprise.

'Robin Judkins.' It was clearly his no-nonsense greeting. I decided to match it and waded in.

'Robin, I'm Kelly Barber and I want to do the Coast to Coast.'

'What's your address?'

I gave it.

'You're on the mailing list, anything else?'

'Um yeah ... I want to get started training and ...'

He cut in. 'Have you ever done any kayaking?'

'No.'

'You need to talk to Don Dawson. I'll get his number.'

He got it.

'Don will look after you. Tell him I sent you. Anything else?'

'No.'

'OK, bye...' He hung up.

I was stunned. I wasn't exactly sure what I expected but a 40-second telephone call wasn't it. I expected more... of something. It had seemed to me – however illogical – that to start off on a huge adventure like the Coast to Coast the first thing you did was spend hours on the phone asking as many questions as you could think of while you received a great many patient answers. If Mr Judkins shared my enthusiasm he certainly didn't show it. (Much later it occurred to me that organising an event with a thousand or so competitors was not achieved by spending long periods of time on the phone discussing minor details of the race with enthusiastic rookies.)

I had also expected that after speaking with him I would have some idea what to do next. I didn't, and I was a trifle annoyed. I still knew nothing bar the fact I was on some sort of mailing list. I was back to square one. All I had was another telephone number.

I decided to dispense with my usual build-up and get on with it. I rang the number and asked for Don.

'Speaking,' was the relaxed reply.

'Don, I'm Kelly Barber and I want to do the Coast to Coast. I phoned Robin Judkins and he told me to talk to you.'

'Have you done any kayaking?' Don asked.

It was starting to sound like I had stumbled upon a secret organisation. The code words were obviously 'have you done any kayaking', and the appropriate answer was quite clearly 'no'.

Don, it turned out, was a pretty interesting bloke. He had done the

Coast to Coast a few times and he especially enjoyed kayaking. In fact he had a few different kayaks and if I wanted I could come around some time and have a look at them. If I wanted, maybe I could even take one out.

I was very excited.

'Don, I know it's kind of short notice but can I come around now?'

'Sure.'

'Thanks. I'll see you soon.'

A few moments later I phoned back for the address, and then again a bit later for directions. At least I now had no need to worry about creating a good first impression.

I turned up outside his house another half hour later. It was the last house in the street on the edge of a fair-size park. The park was dotted with well pruned, towering pines that looked a bit like giant mushrooms. A large variety of smaller native New Zealand plants cowered under the canopy, straining upwards for any morsel of sunlight. A stone-chip path wound its way through the undergrowth and off into the distance. It was a beautiful place to live.

Don's house was a simple brick single-story place with a tidy front yard and a couple of healthy-looking ngaio trees dominating the view from the street. With no branches under head height the trees provided excellent shade and unobstructed westerly views of the Southern Alps from the large windows at the front of the house.

You simply could not live in this house and not think about kayaking. Just beyond the front lawn, about as far as you could spit in a gentle following breeze, was a river. It was wide enough that you couldn't throw a stone to the other side.

With so many trees surrounding the nearest houses off in the distance you could be forgiven for imagining there was nothing between you and the mountains but open land. It was paradise.

But I was on a mission. A quick survey of the front of the house told me either I was blind or there was no front door, so I strode purposefully around the back. I found a likely-looking door and knocked. A woman opened it, smiled and invited me in. Her name was Margaret and in no time I was sitting at her kitchen table with a cup of tea. Margaret excused herself and disappeared to the other end of the house. She soon returned with a chap she introduced as her husband, Don.

Don was a sprightly older man with short hair and a well-trimmed grey beard. I guessed he was in his mid to late 50s but it was difficult to say for certain. He shook my hand with a big grin and sat down.

'So you want to do the Coast to Coast.'

I explained my side of the story. I was pretty excited about the whole thing and probably babbled on a bit too long, but Don didn't seem to mind. We chatted away for an hour or so and I found him excellent company. He sure as heck knew a sight more about everything to do with the Coast to Coast than I did, and he didn't mind my many questions. I had a sneaking suspicion that he thought I was young, keen and dumber than a post, but despite that I thought we got on well.

Don seemed to know everybody. He was not only a personal friend of Judkins but he threw into the conversation the names of all sorts of people I'd never heard of. I was impressed. Even more impressive was the fact that Don had done the race twelve times, and what's more he hadn't even done the first one until he was 50 years old. That made him at least 62 years old. I couldn't see it. I realized I knew little of the activities of 60-year-olds. I guess I imagined them sitting at home knitting doilies and drooling onto the TV guide. Neither he nor Margaret, who was around the same age, drooled on anything the entire time I was there and I saw no evidence of doily production whatsoever.

Throughout my visit Margaret kept up a consistent barrage of cakes, biscuits and scones and I was pretty sure I wouldn't need to eat for the next few days. It just didn't seem polite to refuse. Eventually – perhaps when she was getting dangerously low on cakes – Margaret suggested Don take me out to have a look at his kayaks. I guessed she was going to use the opportunity to do some more baking in case Don and I felt faint from hunger on our return from the garage.

The kayak rack was behind the garage. It was an ingenious little rack that looked like two ladders set a few metres apart. Suspended between them on each of five rungs was a kayak. They did not look quite like the kayaks I remembered from whenever it was that I last saw one up close. For a start they were much longer than I expected. I mentioned this to Don and he said I was probably thinking about canoes. Together we pulled the top one out of the rack and carefully placed it on his back lawn.

It sure was long. Don said it was 5.2 metres, or about 17 feet. The front of the kayak came to a point like a sharp blade. From here the front deck widened before gradually sloping up and then steeply dropping away to the cockpit. It looked similar to a single-seater race car with its cramped cockpit and small dash. Behind the seat the body narrowed back to a stubby point. Perched on the end was a rudder. An ingeniously simple affair, it had a narrow metal base that sat on the tail of the kayak while the blade hung out and over the stern. At the top of the blade was a small wing and blade direction was obviously controlled by a cord attached to each side of the wing. These disappeared a few inches away into the torso of the kayak and were attached to pedals in the cockpit.

I observed that the kayak didn't appear to be made of plastic. Don frowned. He explained that being so light and strong, these days Kevlar was generally the preferred material for racing kayaks. I had no idea what Kevlar was but decided to let it go for the present. I was hoping to take a kayak out and I was mildly concerned too many more of my 'astute' observations might see an end to that.

Don put me at ease by telling me I could take one of the 'boats', as he called them, any time I felt the urge, whether he or Margaret were home or not. I was surprised at his generosity. This was great news indeed. I was keen to go out immediately, but Don explained I still had a few things to learn.

The kayak he pulled out of the rack was called a Sprinter. I noted that it was very narrow and looked quick. Don confirmed this was an accurate observation and explained it was a boat for advanced kayakers. Narrow boats draw less water and therefore go faster, but they tend to sacrifice stability, so that, like on a bicycle, if you are not moving forward then you are falling over. Any sudden shift of weight or crisis of balance can see you upside-down quite suddenly. The change in view and temperature can be very unwelcome.

I also learnt that while the average person might be able to successfully paddle a narrow boat on a body of calm water, the realities of kayaking in the Coast to Coast are quite different. The Waimakariri River is not calm. It is alive. An incessant flow of hidden energy and subdued activity, it simmers away quietly but reacts violently when narrowing banks or obstacles impede its progress.

In narrow or 'tippy' boats, as they are aptly named, the kayaker is constantly being pushed off balance by the movement of the water as it careers down its course over rocks and unseen boulders below the surface. It takes skill and experience to read the tell-tale clues on the surface water and then respond with the subtle shifts in balance and paddle-stroke required to stay upright. There is no substitute for experience on the water.

On the other hand, wide-bottomed boats like the plastic canoes I was familiar with are very stable and forgiving. Because they are so wide they are less likely to tip and are more like a tricycle than a two-wheeled bike. Energy can be spent on moving forward rather than on staying upright. But with this stability comes the sacrifice of an awful lot of speed.

The trick, according to Don, was to find the boat that matched my skill. He said a slow, wide boat might take me ten minutes longer to paddle down the river but would easily beat someone paddling a quicker boat if they didn't have the skills to keep it upright. With this in mind Don took another kayak out of the rack. It was called a Challenger. If the Sprinter was a speedboat the Challenger was a barge.

In my excitement it was all the same to me. I just wanted to get out on the water and start paddling, but Don kept introducing new pieces of equipment.

The spray skirt was aptly named. I put it on and initially felt rather sheepish. It was like an oddly shaped woman's skirt. Made of neoprene rubber, like a surfing or diving wetsuit, it was shaped to stretch and fit over the cockpit rim. When attached it would ensure the kayak was pretty much airtight and water could not enter and flood the main chamber, sinking the boat. Don explained that if a kayaker is tipped upside down in the water it is quite a simple matter, once taught, to right oneself by completing an 'Eskimo roll.' To stay focused I put aside all thoughts of what an Eskimo roll might taste like. I sure was learning valuable stuff here.

Next he gave me some slip-on rubber-soled shoes and a lifejacket. I surveyed the jacket with interest. It was more of a vest than a jacket and it had an array of clips and pockets for as yet unknown purposes. I slipped it on. It felt awkward and uncomfortable until Don pointed out that I had it on backwards. Once on the right way it was surprisingly comfortable and I noticed there was ample room to move my arms. No doubt this was so I could freely flail about with the most crucial piece of equipment: the paddle.

Don grabbed one from a rack he had next to the kayaks. I'd seen paddles before but this one was quite different. For a start its blade was not flat, but shaped like a long scoop. This seemed to me to make sense. I could imagine it pulling the water like the cupped hand of a swimmer.

Finally I had everything I needed to go for my first paddle. I whipped out to the car for my shorts and a T-shirt, and changed in the garage. Don showed me how to sling the kayak over my shoulder and I walked the short distance to the river and got in. In no time I was off paddling, a grin from ear to ear and happy as a loon.

The Challenger was anything but a challenge and I had no trouble at all keeping it upright. In fact I was pretty confident I could just about stand up in the thing. I paddled for an hour. I had such a great time I failed to notice that my entire upper body had gotten wet.

I hosed the boat down on my return, thanked Don and drove home. I felt triumphant. I had learnt a lot, paddled a kayak and met a multisport guru. I had even done some training. I also knew where I could get a seemingly limitless supply of cakes and biscuits. They were small steps, but I was on my way.

Chapter 3

Fear and Loathing

A couple of days later a very official-looking letter arrived with a Speight's Coast to Coast logo in the top right-hand corner. Among an extraordinary number of flyers for adventure clothing and equipment, I was delighted to find an entry form. As I went through it I began to get excited. Finally, this was it! Concrete details. I realised that apart from Don's vague descriptions of what the river section was like and roughly where it went, I knew little of the route and virtually nothing of the actual detail of the race.

Now things would be different. I would read the entry form, then I would prepare my body and turn it into the machine required to do what I asked of it. There would be no looking back. I would simply train myself and then conquer. I sat daydreaming for some time, before drifting back to reality.

The form started innocently enough. I had to register the day before the race at the Kumara Racecourse, which could be found a short distance west of the township of Kumara by following the main road.

I got up from my desk to find Kumara on the map of New Zealand's South Island on my wall. There it was: a tiny town on the edge of the island. I looked more closely at the names of the surrounding towns and realised I had been that way before. I searched my mind for an impression of what the place looked like. I could not picture the town.

Kumara, it seems, was one of those towns you barely noticed as you rushed by on the way to more important destinations. It hadn't always been so.

According to legend, in June of 1876 a number of gentlemen with a fondness for illicit whiskey were digging out foundations for their still on the banks of the Taramakau River when they struck gold. As chance would have it at the time there were a large number of prospecting parties already scouring the area for gold and so the town of Kumara sprang to life. The Kumara diggings, as they were known, attracted the usual array of fortune seekers from far and wide including an exceptional man by the name of Richard John Seddon, who, having put his experience on the Victorian goldfields to good use by investing in stores in Hokitika, 30 kilometres from Kumara, and becoming one of the few people to make any real money out of the gold rush, went on to win the job of Kumara's first mayor and eventually made his way to the office of Prime Minister.

'King Dick', as he was known, was a legend. He was stubborn, rugged and ruthless, a forceful speaker and a man who demanded loyalty. Seddon had many foibles but he was a man of the people, with a great and genuine love of humanity. Among other things, under his leadership New Zealand became the first country in the world to grant women the vote. Personally Seddon was opposed to the idea, but there are none like politicians for jumping on the winning side of an argument.

If Kumara was the political birthplace of one of New Zealand's most memorable political careers then it would be the birthplace of my journey too.

According to the entry form the race proper was due to start the day after registration, on Kumara Beach at 7am. I thought 7am was a tad early but couldn't imagine anyone changing it for me. The entry form stated that competitors were expected to run 2.8 kilometres from the beach to where our bikes would be waiting for us. I thought this quite manageable, and read on feeling rather confident.

Competitors would then cycle 55 kilometres to the first checkpoint, where we would hand our bikes over to our assistants, who would have travelled on ahead. Fifty-five kilometres! That seemed like rather a long way. I tried to imagine biking 55 kilometres, but it had been so long since I had been any distance on a bike at all that it was difficult to relate to. Then I remembered a long bike ride I had done as a youth. A friend and I had decided to bike to a picnic spot where our two families would meet for lunch. It was about 35 kilometres from home. We rode out there full of youthful enthusiasm but at a leisurely pace. It took about 3 hours. We had such a splendid afternoon that when it came time to go home my friend and I decided, in the spirit of adventure and using the widely celebrated wisdom of the teenage mind, that biking home would also be an excellent idea.

With no preparation and an already full day of physical activity under our belts we soon began to suffer greatly. We biked on and on. At times I wondered if we would ever get home but we finally dragged our sorry arses the last few kilometres. We had ended up taking four and a half hours for the return journey, arriving in the dark. Most of the next day I slept.

I did some quick math. Based on the trials of my youth it was quite conceivable that to bike the 55 kilometres in the first leg of the race could take me six or seven hours. With that sobering thought reverberating around my head I read on.

After I had handed my bike to my assistant I could commence the final section of the day – the run. Virtually the first act of the run was to cross the Otira River.

I sat up a little. Cross a river! Even a non-adventurer such as myself knew that crossing rivers had its dangers.

New Zealand, with its abundance of popular and often easily accessible mountain tracks and trails, has seen more than enough drowning deaths over the years as a result of hikers attempting to cross often benign-looking rivers and streams. In fact drowning at river crossings is the single biggest cause of death in the mountains. From time to time reports come out of hikers losing their footing and cartwheeling end over end and out of sight around the next bend while their friends watch in horror.

I decided that when the time came I would follow the majority of other competitors, whom I sincerely hoped would be all around me.

After the river crossing I saw that I would then proceed to run up the Deception Valley and cross the Main Divide of the Southern Alps at Goat Pass, at a height of 1,070 metres.

Reading it quickly it didn't sound so bad. I was a trifle concerned at the name Goat Pass, however. In my experience place names are deservedly assigned and this one conjured up images of treacherous rocky slopes and other kinds of places I had no wish to visit. One would hardly venture into Death Valley looking for a lush green paddock. Similarly, I'm not sure I would want to take my young children for a Sunday stroll on a nearby mountain known as the Devil's Backbone. I have never seen the place, it could be a cakewalk, but I doubt it.

Assuming I managed to negotiate Goat Pass I was then expected to run down the Mingha Valley, crossing various rivers and streams as they presented themselves in their fury, before what I could only imagine would be a painful limp toward the end of that section at a picnic spot called Klondyke Corner.

The form gaily announced the distance as 33 kilometres. This completed day one.

I felt ill. It was finally dawning on me the enormity of what it was I was hoping to do. As I read on my confidence waned and it was not long before I started to have serious doubts. I kept reading in search of hope but I found none.

The form stated joyfully that toward the end of day one competitors' assistants establish a tent camp, and as competitors arrive they are timed in and spend the night at the camp. My major concerns had begun to revolve around not when I would arrive to get timed in but if. My confidence continued to suffer in light of the enormous challenges I was going to have to face. Every new piece of information seemed to shout at me: 'You're nuts, how did you think you could ever do such a thing? Take a look in the mirror. It's only you.' It was true: it was only me.

I thought about this as I scanned through a few more of the race details. I realized I had to change my mindset. If I was going to cope with this journey then the first step was going to have to be to win the battle in my mind.

I phoned Don. He wasn't home but Margaret was.

'What's wrong?'

She was a perceptive woman.

'I'm crapping myself. I don't think I can do this.'

I told her about my concerns. The river, the distance, Goat Pass, 7 hours of biking, 33 kilometres, pain, fear and loathing.

Margaret was a veteran. She had heard it all before, probably from Don. She told me to relax and then gave me the single most useful piece of advice I have ever been given: 'Others have done it and so can you. It always seems worse than it is.'

I hung up feeling a lot better, and returned to the entry form.

On the run section I was required to carry a daypack with warm clothing, wet-weather gear, a full set of polypropylene (warm underwear), food, drink, a first-aid kit, a survival blanket and a map of the area. It seemed like an awful lot of extra gear. I half-expected the next paragraph of compulsory gear to require one small satellite dish, one Kalashnikov assault rifle, and a liferaft to seat twelve.

Reading on, a couple of curious sentences initially confused me. They were printed in bold type. One stated that no dogs were allowed. It seemed odd to specifically exclude them. (I noted llamas weren't mentioned. I hear they make good pets.) I couldn't understand why anyone would want to take a dog anyway but just in case I was thinking of taking one, there it was in black and white: No!

The next sentence was a bit harsh too and stated that any competitor who dropped rubbish on the mountain run would be disqualified.

I suspected the hand of officialdom lurking in the background. I soon found it.

'The Department of Conservation requires that etc etc ... in order to protect the ecological values of the area and the recreational experiences of other users.' Aha! The Department of Conservation. That could only mean that the race course passed through a national park.

Like many countries New Zealand has large tracts of land that are designated national parks. These areas are generally chosen for their special beauty and grandeur. They are sanctuaries for plant and animal life, created so that for generations to come visitors will be able to enjoy an area of protected and largely untouched land. In addition, some of this land is designated a 'Wilderness Area'. Wilderness areas are generally wholly untouched pieces of land where there exist particularly interesting vegetation and wildlife and where no development is permitted, in an attempt to retain as much of the natural landscape as possible. If you were, for instance, to find a family of yeti living in a particularly quiet corner of a national park and existing largely on a diet of grasses that were previously thought to be extinct it is quite likely that in a short while it would be designated a Wilderness Area.

Most people in New Zealand think national parks are a good idea. So good, in fact, that national parks are protected in law by the National Parks Act. This ensures that the parks belong in perpetuity to all the people of New Zealand and that no sneaky bastard can come along and build an airport in the middle of the place just because the views on take-off would be excellent.

Of course if you are going to have all these national parks you are going to need to look after them, especially if the general public is going to crawl all over them getting lost and falling off mountains and so on. In New Zealand this is taken care of by the Department of Conservation.

They are an interesting lot. Many are outdoors people. In my experience they are hard-working and committed people who love what they do and where they do it. If you consider how many people use New Zealand's national parks and their oftentimes very inhospitable environments, and how few problems they encounter, you can understand just how good the DOC staff are, despite the inherent bureaucracy in a government department.

One of the true mysteries of the Speight's Coast to Coast is how Judkins, with his firebrand personality and a long-time dislike of bureaucracy, managed to bite his tongue long enough to get the necessary dispensations to run a commercial event in a national park. That Judkins and DOC have managed to work together for many years to ensure the national icon that is the Coast to Coast continues, is a credit to both parties.

Day two looked interesting. For a start it would begin at the more civilised time of 7.30am. Groups of 10 cyclists would depart at one-minute intervals and cycle the 15 kilometres to the river. I immediately saw the logic: hundreds of competitors arriving at the river to launch themselves into their kayaks at the same time would be chaos on a grand scale. I imagined competitors rushing around in a frenzy looking for misplaced gear while their support crews jostled each other aggressively for a spot at the water's edge to launch their kayak. I imagined the highly competitive, charged-up atmosphere causing a few bumps, trips and the occasional accidental whack from carelessly swung paddles. I imagined a bit of shouting and swearing and a few scuffles and the inevitable brawl. I imagined the bewildered competitors paddling off to face the river while agitated support crews milled about, trying to calm down. I imagined it all. Judkins must have too. Starting them in groups of 10, a minute apart, was really smart.

At the end of this short cycle section I would leave my bicycle and amble down a dirt road to my kayak, which was apparently going to be waiting for me. It occurred to me that someone was going to have to get up rather early to put it there but I knew it wasn't going to be me so I dismissed the thought.

Once I arrived at the kayak I would be faced with the simple matter of getting into my gear and kayaking a mere 67 kilometres down the Waimakariri River.

I knew nothing of the Waimakariri River. Well, that's not entirely true. I had passed over the very eastern end of it (nowhere near the portion that is used in the race) a few times on my way to somewhere or other, but like much of the scenery when I'm driving I seldom gave it my attention, except to note that from time to time it took on an ugly brown muddy colour, as if it were the Ganges. It had seldom looked safe or inviting. Even on the hottest days.

I had recently visited the local library for books on the area through which the race passed. I pulled them out and began to scan them for references to the river. There was very little but I did find one story that was a trifle unsettling. I was reading of the adventures of two young university students, Mr G.N. Carrington and Mr B. Wyn-Irwin, in the early 1920s. These fine young adventurers had spent every opportunity their studies allowed exploring the area that was to eventually become the Arthur's Pass National Park. They bravely climbed many of the local mountain peaks, and their enthusiasm for the challenges of the area provided much of the inspiration for the founding of the Canterbury Mountaineering Club. At this point I stumbled across a nasty surprise. It seems that despite surviving some of the most difficult peaks in the area, the young Mr Carrington had tragically drowned during an attempt to raft the gorge section of the Waimakariri River.

Cheered up no end, I went back to the entry form, and there it was – a rather minimal description of the river section: 'Competitors set off down 25 kilometres of flat, braided river before entering 25 kilometres of the gorge, which is rated as a grade two stretch of river.' It went on: 'The gorge will be patrolled by jet boats.' That was a relief. Too late for the brave Mr Carrington but welcome nevertheless. From there, competitors would kayak 17 kilometres of flat, braided river to the transition point at the Gorge Bridge and the end of stage three. The form glibly stated that the kayak section should take from four to eight hours, and highly recommended a practice trip down the river.

All that followed, I read, was a pleasant 70-kilometre jaunt on my bike to the final destination of Sumner Beach.

Finally all I had to do was decide whether to do the race in one day or two. It was an easy decision. The one-day race was for the elite. For me, doing it over two days would be difficult enough. I totalled up the distances. 243 kilometres. Wow!

When I took it all in I wondered if I hadn't bitten off more than I could chew. Way, way more than I could chew. But then again, if I applied a bit of Margaret's logic to the situation then surely I had a good chance. If others had done the Coast to Coast then I could too. It wasn't going to be easy but I was going to do it.

I took a small piece of paper and wrote:

2.8-km run
55-km bike
33-km run
Sleep
15-km bike
67-km kayak
70-km bike
Victory

I pinned the piece of paper to the wall at the end of the bed. I lay down and looked at it for a while. Now I knew my adversary.

Chapter 4

Learning to Kayak

Over the next few weeks I was often around at Don's. I would paddle for about an hour, clean the gear I had used, thank Don if he was about, maybe if invited have a cup of tea and a chat, and then take off home. We talked about the Coast to Coast and ate a hell of a lot of cakes and biscuits. I learnt a great deal. I felt I was getting the hang of things rather quickly and Don made me feel good when he mentioned casually in a rare moment of praise that my paddle stroke was pretty darn good for a beginner.

I was beginning to think that perhaps I had even underestimated my abilities, when one day I turned up at Don's and one of his other kayaks was already out on the lawn waiting for me. Don had an odd sort of smirk on his face that I didn't like the look of, so I turned my attention to the boat.

It was disturbingly narrow. Even more disturbing was the fact that it didn't have a rudder. Don said it was called a Vision and since I seemed to be doing so well I should give it a shot and see how I got on.

I said this seemed fair enough but that I had a few concerns about the complete lack of steering apparatus. Don explained a kayak could be quite successfully directed by leaning to one side, which would gently steer it in the opposite direction to the lean. He went on to say that if my rudder ever broke then this would be my only way of getting home.

I took the Vision down to the water, got in and paddled carefully away from the bank. It was a nightmare. I felt like I was trying to ride a bike with no handlebars on a tightrope. I could barely balance the kayak, let alone steer it. To make matters worse I had forgotten to put on the spray skirt and the cold water was flicking off the paddle onto my bare legs. I was very soon wet, cold and annoyed with myself. The muscles in my buttocks, thighs and hips were doing overtime as I twitched violently one way then the next in a desperate attempt to maintain control and stay upright.

I slowly began to weave my way up the river. Anyone looking from the bank might think I had gotten totally drunk, stolen the kayak and was now trying to make some form of getaway. Not that I would have noticed anyone watching. I was lost in a Zombie-like focus, looking straight ahead at nothing in particular, afraid that if I looked anywhere other than straight ahead of me I would lose balance and tip over. I was right.

A few minutes downriver, exhausted from all the balancing, I stole a quick look at a passing cyclist on the riverbank and over I went. The cold water was a shock to the system but it wasn't more than three feet deep and the current was slow so I was able to scramble out as the boat began filling with water. In my initial panic to escape a watery grave I managed to whack my shin on the edge of the cockpit. I let out a frustrated yell.

I stood in waist-deep water, wet, haggard and cold, with a paddle in one hand and a half-submerged kayak in the other, contemplating my next move. I resolved to empty the kayak and carry on. I began to walk the few yards to the riverbank when I stepped into a large hole and went under again. I thrashed around a bit for good measure as I tried to regain my feet and soon found shallow water and eventually the bank, where I could put the paddle down and devote two hands to emptying the kayak. I struggled with the weight of the water inside but eventually managed to get most of it out. Within minutes of doing so I was determinedly afloat and cautiously twitching my way back up the river, back in my role as the drunken thief.

As I improved and grew in confidence I discovered that Don was right. If I leaned ever so gently to one side the kayak would slowly begin to veer away from the direction of my lean. I matched the lean on the other side and the kayak returned to where it started. I found that the better I got at doing this the more successful I became at travelling in a straight line. I was beginning to think that to the casual observer it might look as if I'd had just a couple of drinks and not the whole bottle.

I had a few more tricky moments but got back to Don's place without further incident. I cleaned up, then found Don and told him of my adventure. He said he and Margaret had enjoyed watching it from the front window.

I decided not to charge them for the entertainment and went home to lick my wounds.

I knew I had to persist with the kayaking caper if I was ever going to survive the actual race so a few days later when Don invited me out for a Sunday afternoon paddle with a friend I eagerly accepted. Don took his Sprinter and I wobbled off beside him in the Vision. Not far past his house and the park the river widened, went under a large road bridge and then widened even further into an estuary. The tide was full as we paddled out towards the middle. It wasn't long before we saw someone paddling toward us from the other side of the estuary and shortly afterwards I met Sharon. As far as I could make out Sharon was a bit older than I but not as old as Don. She had black hair cut to a practical length and a welcoming grin. When she spoke I could see she had a certain self-confidence. She nodded in my direction on introduction and then floated up beside me and whispered, 'So the old boy's got a new disciple has he?' I liked her immediately.

She was clearly a good paddler. She spun her Sprinter around like an expert and I marvelled that anyone could have so much control over such a narrow boat. We headed off toward a corner of the estuary and while Don and Sharon chatted away I started to drift behind. I was thankful that there was little wind, but I still had problems balancing and steering the kayak at the same time. Every now and then Don would turn around to see how I was getting on. The first time he looked I was just over his left shoulder. I half-smiled and nervously got back to concentrating. He turned back and continued his conversation.

A few minutes later he looked around and I wasn't there. I could see him searching for me and wondering where the hell I'd got to. Somehow I had shifted balance and got stuck going to the right. I couldn't correct it. How was he to know I was now about 200 feet on the other side of him? I risked a dunking and threw my body around in the kayak. The move had the desired effect and I now found I could steer left rather well. Too well in fact. All I could do was go left. I couldn't go right at all, and I certainly couldn't go in a straight line. I felt like a contortionist as I twisted my body this way and that trying to get some semblance of control over the beast. It was infuriating.

'Have you done any kayaking?' Don Dawson, multisport guru, shows that he has. Paul's Camera Shop

I decided I needed to discuss my predicament with Don so I set out to catch up to him. This was easier said than done. The kayak decided not to come and immediately set off to the right. I paddled furiously, only making a stroke on the right side. After about 20 strokes I had made no progress to the left but had managed to travel more or less in a straight line. It was a small victory.

By the time I had started to close in on Don and Sharon I figured I had paddled at least twice as far as they had in the same time. As they enjoyed their leisurely paddle across the estuary I paddled furiously behind them, weaving wildly from side to side. I was sweating like a pig and my heart was pounding. It was becoming a hell of a workout.

Quite suddenly I lost balance and went over.

Time stood still. I realized my predicament. I was upside down in about eight feet of water, in the middle of an estuary, a mile from the shore. What the hell was I going to do? If I ripped the spray skirt off, how was I going to get back in the kayak? There was nowhere to stand up – it was too deep.

Quite simply, I was stuffed.

Then all my years of watching television finally paid off and I had a vision. I recalled a scene in which I had seen a man in a canoe roll himself upright by flashing his paddle around in a sideways motion. It had been filmed underwater. I remembered it as if I had just seen it. Without thinking I thrashed my paddle sideways in a wild panic and at the same time threw my hips around and backwards and I was up.

I was stunned. I yelled triumphantly at the top of my lungs. The adrenaline flowed through my veins and I felt alive like never before.

I had absolutely no idea how I had rolled upright and I didn't care either.

Don and Sharon had stopped at the yell and looked around to see me beaming away as I paddled confidently towards them. I now felt oddly relaxed, and it seemed to have affected my paddling. I was less cautious and jittery in my movements and even managed to get some semblance of control over my direction. However, just before my triumphant arrival beside Don and Sharon I stroked too hard on the left side, lost balance and went over again.

I threw the panic switch and thrashed about in the same manner as the last time. I didn't even break the surface. Since my last success had been more of a fortuitous spasm than a planned action I had no real technique to build on.

I tried again. This time I got halfway up, gasped in a breath, before going back under. I managed to catch a brief glimpse of Don and the startled look on his face. I wondered what he was thinking. I decided to have one last shot at resurfacing. I was preparing to spasm as violently as possible when the paddle struck the bottom and I realized I was in shallow water.

I pushed off the bottom and was soon upright again. It wasn't quite as graceful as the last time but I wasn't complaining. Don was beside himself and laughing violently. Perhaps he hadn't been as concerned as he first looked.

'You should have seen the first one,' I gasped between breaths.

'You mean you went over before this?' Don replied.

'Yeah, it was a real beauty.'

'Where did you learn to roll?'

'About a hundred yards back there,' I said, nodding behind me.

Don was impressed. I could see him revising his assessment of me. It was clear he wasn't too sure where I now fitted in.

Safely back on shore we decided that kayaking without a rudder in a narrow boat was best left to others. Don said he had an idea of the boat I should purchase. It had enough stability to give me confidence and it would be pretty quick as well. He offered to get one from a friend of his for me to try out. Things were looking up.

That night as I lay in bed, in the half light I could see the note I had put on the wall. I read it again.

2.8-km run
55-km bike
33-km run
Sleep
15-km bike
67-km kayak
70-km bike
Victory

The 2.8-kilometre run I could handle. The sleep part was easy too. I had been training for it for years. And although I had been paddling on the tamest water imaginable I was at least part-way to the goal of the 67-kilometre kayak. I rated my confidence in finishing the event at four out of 10 and building. I was feeling pretty good.

I fell asleep and into a hideous dream of kayaking down the Waimakariri River in waves and rapids as big as houses and swirling whirlpools that sucked in whole trees and ripped off their branches. I fell out of my boat, got smashed against rocks and was held under water for what seemed like an eternity before I woke in a sweat. I turned on the light and read my Bible for the first time in ages.

The kayak Don had in mind for me was called an Eclipse. It was basic and stable but it was also relatively quick. Within a week of his suggestion Don had borrowed an Eclipse for me to try. He seemed to have an inexhaustible supply of friends who would part with whatever it was he wanted to borrow at the drop of a hat.

After the array of boats I had already tried at Don's request the Eclipse was a dream. I fell in love with it. For the first time I felt truly confident in a kayak. It handled well, seemed as stable as a pontoon and felt like it was always going faster than anything else I had tried. I knew it was the boat for me.

I immediately resolved to buy one for myself as soon as possible and told Don. He grinned. He said it was probably the right choice but he also explained that unfortunately a hell of a lot of other people thought the same thing and therefore procuring an Eclipse at the right price was not an easy task. A new one was going to cost somewhere around $2500.

I had other problems. One was the formidable task of not attracting the attention of my wife. I decided I could realistically expect to spend about $2000 on both a kayak and a bike and stay married. I also decided that of the two the kayak would have to be my priority.

Early one Friday afternoon I spotted a small advertisement that announced FOR SALE ECLIPSE KAYAK. GOOD CONDITION. PH ———. I phoned immediately, only to be greeted by an answer machine. Without intending to sound too desperate I left a rather desperate message saying I had been looking for an Eclipse for a while and for the owner to call me first as soon as they got home. The message had the desired effect and a little over an hour later I was knocking at the door of the Eclipse owner's home. He was about my age and had decided that his pending business commitments were likely to see the end of his athletics days for a few years. He had decided to shed some of his superfluous equipment. I was the first vulture to land on the carcass.

We popped down to his garage to see the kayak. It was beautiful. Its long, sleek shape glistened in the dim garage light. It had a shiny finish and had obviously been well looked after. I immediately felt real excitement about my prospects for completing the Coast to Coast and I knew that it was this boat that was going to make my dream a possibility.

Of course, despite my gushy and unmanly feelings for the kayak, I tried to display none of this on my face. I wanted to appear as if I had seen a thousand kayaks just like this one. I wanted it to seem like this boat was nothing special and that in fact I'd seen so many better ones that I was clearly wasting my time here. But I couldn't. I ran my hands all over the boat and excitedly asked a whole range of questions about it. The owner responded to my enthusiasm and we talked for an hour.

I thought I had certainly blown any chance of getting a bargain. I had the poker face of a clown and I couldn't stop grinning. These feelings soon gave way to worry. It dawned on me that this little beauty that I simply had to have was going to take up so much of my $2000 kayak/bike fund that I was only going to be able to afford a child's bicycle.

I needn't have worried. Realising I was just an excited novice, in an extraordinary gesture the owner gave me the kayak for $1600 and threw in airbags and a few other bits and pieces as well. I was ecstatic. I was especially pleased with the airbags, which fitted in the back of the kayak to keep it afloat should it tip upside down.

Getting the Eclipse at such a price was not only a great deal but an example of the generosity I was seeing in the people I met on my adventure.

I had one more thing to do before I passed final judgement on the Eclipse. I took the kayak home, got my gear organised and went down to the river. I paddled out and blasted around for twenty minutes or so. It was everything I had hoped it would be. Although the Avon River barely has a ripple in it at the best of times, the Eclipse felt as if it would be stable in rougher water. In fact it felt at least as stable as Don's old Challenger, yet it was also noticeably faster. I had yet to test it in white water, but I left the river feeling quite sure I had the right boat for my adventure.

Chapter 5

It's All About the Bike

One beautifully sunny Saturday morning I decided it was a perfect day to begin my cycle training. The only problem of course was that I didn't own a bike. It was such a nice day I decided to ignore this fact and begin anyway.

I knew just the trick. I crashed around in the garage for a while until I found what I was looking for: my wife's prehistoric mountain bike. It was a beauty. I had bought it for her birthday around the time the first mountain bikes began appearing. She rode it to work until she got pregnant and the bike was subsequently retired to the nether regions of the garage and forgotten. And here it was – handlebars sticking out of a pile of old household junk, a bit dusty and dirty but otherwise in good condition. It looked a sturdy beast with its full-size frame, large wheels and gnarled black tyres.

In fact it was so sturdy I had considerable trouble lifting it out of its spot at the rear of the garage. Not only was it was as heavy as an anvil but it also seemed to be attached to almost everything surrounding it.

I swore at it. I kicked it. I fought viciously to wrench it out. Bathed in sweat and mad as hell, I stopped to rest. Then I noticed what I hadn't seen before. An old dark-green hose horribly tangled in the back wheel. I knew just what to do. After two minutes, clipping with the hedge trimmers I managed to wrestle the bike free.

I also found an old dusty bike helmet. It was bright yellow and was shaped like an American GI helmet but it was all I had so I put it on. I was ready to ride.

I creaked down the driveway and out on to the street. It was great. I had forgotten how much fun it was riding a bike. In no time I built up speed and was flying along.

Cycling around the city for a couple of hours, I discovered a few things. Cycling was hard work. While it wasn't anywhere near as exhausting as running, it still required more effort than I had imagined. I realised I would have to put plenty of time into training.

I became aware of another curious fact: most other cyclists ignored me. As they passed on the other side of the road I would offer a wave or a smile and nod a greeting but they'd seldom respond, even if they'd been looking directly at me. The serious cyclists were the worst. They would slope past, hunched low over their glistening, space-age bikes, adorned in brightly coloured, body-hugging Lycra and sporting the monikers of foreign professional race teams. They would turn their heads for a moment and briefly scan me through lightly-tinted specialised cycling glasses. I would wave. They would turn away and were gone.

I didn't understand. Was I a leper? Here I was, a fellow cyclist out training for my big race and trying to be polite while my fellow cyclists looked through me as if I was a pane of glass. Joggers were not like this at all. Neither were kayakers. Sometimes out on the river passing kayakers had even stopped for a chat. Others almost always exchanged pleasantries. But not cyclists.

I began to think rather negatively about the cycling fraternity. In fact I began to think I had discovered the biggest bunch of self-absorbed prats on the planet. After another one passed on the other side of the road without so much as a flicker of reaction to my wave I started to get really annoyed. Their behaviour just wasn't neighbourly. It became my personal mission to get a response.

When the next cyclist appeared I yelled out 'howdy' and waved. He looked across but neither spoke nor waved. He was followed a few minutes later by another cyclist who looked about in surprise at my greeting but didn't seem to see me and certainly didn't acknowledge my greeting.

I was beginning to wonder if perhaps I was now somehow invisible. As if to confirm my theory the next two cyclists ignored me completely. Now I was angry.

I decided on a little experiment. As the next cyclist passed I yelled out 'Plonker!' as loud as I could. He didn't even look up. I arrived home disappointed.

After I'd put the bike away I happened to pass a full-length mirror in the hallway and caught a glimpse of myself. I stopped and went back. Suddenly I understood why the serious cyclists hadn't acknowledged me. I didn't look like them at all. I looked like an idiot.

Either I had to go cycling with my own kind – chubby guys wearing shorts and T-shirts in bright yellow GI helmets – or I had to get some flash cycling clothes. In light of the fact that I had only seen one other fat guy even remotely dressed like me all morning, and because there were likely to be even fewer guys like me in a race like the Coast to Coast, I decided it was time to go shopping. I needed some respectable cycling clothes.

That night, while my dearly beloved wife was out at a school meeting, I got on the internet for some cheap thrills: I went looking for a flash new cycling outfit. I should have typed in the word 'cycling' but I was thinking about adventure and in my confusion I typed in that word instead. I ambled through the headings until I came across an interesting site.

It was a full of information about hiking, mountaineering and other outdoorsy pastimes. They sold all manner of outdoor equipment: I could buy hiking poles, packs, freeze dried foods, clothing, lightweight pots and pans, towels and cooking stoves that looked like miniature space craft. I was hopelessly engrossed. Ever since I was old enough to cut myself with my first Swiss army knife I had loved outdoor equipment and so it was quite some time before I fortuitously stumbled upon a heading announcing 'Cycling Gear' and remembered why I was there.

I scanned the photos of the products, looking for the perfect top and shorts that would earn me acceptance among the cycling fraternity. I by-passed the entry-level shorts and the top with the large sunflower design across the front. This was definitely not the image I was looking for. I scrolled down further and suddenly saw what I wanted. There in tasteful black and blue was a pair of shorts and a classy top with 'New Zealand' printed across the front. This would do the trick for sure.

With a click of the mouse I had ordered two pairs of shorts and a top. A couple of days later they arrived in my letterbox. In the privacy of my bedroom I tore open the packet and excitedly tried them on. They fitted perfectly – well, almost. I did note that the pressure being exerted on some of the more sensitive parts of the male anatomy might take a little getting used to.

I proudly surveyed myself in the hall mirror and was satisfied. Now all I needed was a half-decent bike and I would be able to pass as a respectable cyclist. Things were looking up.

A few days later I had an opportunity to wander around a few bike shops. It was depressing. Road bikes were not cheap. Some were downright expensive. I even found one that I thought was ambitiously priced at a little under $11,000. The shop owner told me he had already sold two in the previous six months. He invited me to have a closer look at it. I wheeled it out of its rack and pretended to cast a knowing eye over it. It was beautiful. Its every appendage seemed to melt seamlessly into the black carbon-fibre frame. It was so aerodynamic it looked like you could ride it head-on into a hurricane. I lifted it effortlessly off the ground and held it there with only one finger. One of my shoes weighed more than this bike. I lusted over it for a few more minutes before putting it back and leaving the store. There was no reason to torture myself any longer.

The following weekend I scanned the local papers and found a couple of pages of cycles for sale. It seemed half the city was trying to rid itself of unwanted cycles. One add in particular caught my eye. The advertisement said TRIATHLON BIKE, GOOD CONDITION, SUIT BEGINNER. Most importantly it announced the price as $300.

Later that morning I found myself at the front door of a house on the other side of the city. I knocked and a tall, shifty-looking bloke answered the door. My first inclination was to turn around and run for my life. He had dark slits for eyes and his head hung forward off his shoulders like Riffraff from the Rocky Horror Picture Show. He wore a black T-shirt, black jeans and work boots and his forearms sported tattoos depicting what looked like the four horsemen of the apocalypse. The only conventional aspect of his appearance was a mobile phone in a black leather pouch hanging off his hip (but I was sure that if it rang the tune would be suitably morose).

Ordinarily I wouldn't have trusted him for directions to the house next door but for one small fact: he was a very polite young man. His name was Blake and he turned out to be a soft-spoken bike enthusiast. As a bit of a hobby and for a few extra dollars (probably for his next apocalyptic tattoo) he tidied up and sold bikes.

Leaning against the shed at the back of his house was the bike. It looked pretty basic but was at least tidy. I went for a quick ride down the road. I liked it. The brakes worked well and it ran through the gears like clockwork.

I took it back and offered him $280. The speed with which he accepted and the smile on his face told me I might have offered too much but I didn't mind. I finally had a bike to call my own.

As I lifted it onto my bike rack I noticed it weighed about as much as a suitcase full of shoes. 'Oh well,' I thought to myself. 'You get what you pay for.'

To celebrate, on the way home I stopped in at a bike shop and bought a new helmet. It was full of racy ventilation holes and looked like a fancy cheese grater.

When I got home I retired my wife's mountain bike and helmet back to the nether regions of the garage. I had no use for that stuff any more. I was a serious cyclist now.

Over the next few weeks I began to do a bit of riding. With my flash clothes, new helmet and acceptable bike I felt a lot better about myself. Other riders acknowledged my existence on the road. I began to enjoy myself more and in no time I started to feel quite comfortable after an hour or so in the saddle. I met a few other cyclists. From time to time I would attach myself to small groups as they came past and ride with them wherever they went.

Cycling with other people was fantastic. Not only was it good bunch-riding practice but it was much more enjoyable than riding alone. The miles seemed to fly by. I was starting to get quite fit and found I could go for longer rides.

One morning I was cruising down a gentle hill when there was a muffled bang and a loud hissing sound came from my back wheel. I knew immediately that I'd either run over a snake with a balloon in its mouth or I had a puncture.

I rattled to a halt, got off my bike and looked down at the back wheel just in time to hear the remaining gasps of air hiss their way to freedom. The tyre was now quite flat.

As I stood there looking forlornly at my now-useless bike and wondering what my next move would be I began to realise the full extent of my predicament. Not only was I at the absolute furthest point from home on my intended trip, but I had no repair kit to fix my puncture with. For some reason it had never occurred to me, in my short cycling career, that a spare tube, tyre levers and a pump would be handy things to take with me on long bike rides.

I cursed myself for being so stupid. What the heck was I going to do now? I looked around. There was a farmhouse just down the road and another one beyond. I knew I had only one option. After a short walk and a considerable explanation I managed to convince the elderly lady in the first farmhouse that I was not a drug-crazed lunatic recently escaped from the nearby prison and she allowed me to call my wife. She turned up half an hour later annoyed at having had to leave coffee with her friends.

The next day I decided to visit a local bike shop for a repair kit and spare tubes. I found John's Cycles in New Brighton Mall without too much trouble and wandered in. It was a small shop as shops go but it was absolutely jam-packed full of bicycles, helmets and cycling gear of all sizes and descriptions. Not only all of the floor space was used up, but the walls were also covered with all manner of cycling paraphernalia. I stared in awe. This was definitely the right place. They had everything.

I looked around for help. At the back of the shop was a small workshop area with a concrete floor where a man was deeply engrossed in working on a bike. He looked an interesting character, around 40, about 5 foot 8 but with a solid build, he wore a small cap that covered his remaining hair and an apron covered in greasy stains. He was dark and freckly and appeared to have spent plenty of time outdoors.

He looked in my direction.

'Can I help you, Chief?'

'I was wondering if you could have a quick look at my bike.'

'What's wrong with it?'

'It's got a flat tyre, and I need a pump and some spare tubes.'

'No worries, Chief, when do you need it?' he asked.

'As soon as possible,' I replied. I was hoping to ride again that afternoon.

'Alright, Chief, no worries,' he replied.

John was a shrewd businessman. Each time I asked the price of something I got two answers. First he told me the retail price, then he told me what I could have it for. It's hard not to like someone who does that.

I bought a pump, some spare tubes, a set of tyre levers and some cycle gloves. According to his unique two-tiered pricing system I saved a lot of money.

He replaced my punctured tube in less than two minutes and the whole time he never stopped giving me advice on how to look after the bike. He was brutally honest.

'How much did you pay for it?'

'What?'

'The bike, Chief, the bike.'

'Three hundred dollars.'

'Had you been drinking?'

'No!' I replied, a little indignantly. I explained that I was doing the Coast to Coast and I had to make do with this bike because of maritally-imposed financial constraints. He understood.

'So what do you really think of my bike anyway?' I asked.

'Oh, it's a piece of shit,' he said without raising an eyebrow. 'It's too big for you, it's heavy, the gear is old and worn and all the cables need replacing.'

I sighed. He saw my grimace and grinned.

'Don't worry, Chief. I'll make sure it gets you there.' He paused for a few seconds before he added what he knew I was anxious to hear. 'Oh and it won't cost you the earth.'

Like I said, he was a shrewd businessman.

Chapter 6

Matters of the Sole

I decided my next move should be to get started with running, the final discipline required for the race.

Over the previous years, in an effort to keep at least mildly in shape for the odd game of soccer, I had been for the occasional run, but you would hardly say I was fit. Comparing my kayaking and cycling fitness to my running fitness, however, my running fitness was world-class.

I wasn't sure how long it was since I had last run but I was pretty confident any friendly microbiologist could give me an accurate date based on the array of fungi making their home in my old running shoes. The sight was truly revolting but strangely compelling: there were enough micro-organisms living in there that with just a little organization these shoes could leave the house of their own accord in search of a better life.

Impressed as I was with the shoe colonies, I wanted to run. I prepared a tub of hot water and toxic household cleaners that resulted in the end of all life in the brave colonies of Nike Left and Right. After giving them a spin cycle in the washing machine and a few hours drying in the midday sun I returned Nike Left and Right to their original function and set out on my first run. I hadn't gone far when I began to notice the final death throes of the colonies: with each impact on the pavement there arose a small but plainly visible puff of dust. I was terribly self-conscious as I passed people in the street, but it wasn't long before these too expired.

Considering how long it had been since my last run it wasn't going too badly. I sauntered around a few streets close to home at a slow pace, trying to keep to a speed that would see me go for about 30 minutes. My goal was to build up my endurance over time. I knew in the actual race I would have to run for a few hours and although I could barely comprehend this yet, I maintained Margaret's reasoning that others had done it and so could I.

After what seemed a reasonable time I turned for home, having more or less decided on a course around a large block which I figured would return me to my home in about 30 minutes. When I arrived back in 25 minutes and still felt pretty darn good I decided to stick to my original plan to run for the full 30 minutes. So with five minutes to go I ran off down the street aimlessly to kill the extra time. Soon I was struggling. My mind was no longer focused on any particular course or direction but rather on my watch and how tired I was. I began to suffer. I just wasn't feeling like running anymore. The letterboxes outside each house had flown by before but now the next one seemed like a target I would never reach.

I wanted to stop and sit down. But while I knew I could stop any time I felt like it, I also knew I would not until I had completed what I had set out to do. I hung on to my goal of running for 30 minutes like a desperate punch-drunk boxer hanging on for the bell in the final round. I trudged on. Finally the 30 minutes ticked over and I allowed myself to stop and then to start walking back.

It was glorious. Though I still had a few hundred metres to get back to my front gate, I had largely recovered by the time I had walked half the distance. A feeling of pleasant tiredness washed over me and I began to experience the runner's high. I also began to reflect.

Okay, maybe voluntary discomfort is a silly way to pass your day but I felt that by embracing it, setting my goal and attaining it, I had conquered something powerful. I wasn't entirely sure what it was I had conquered but whatever it was, I had done it with a willpower I had seldom bothered to awaken before. I was, however, puzzled over my sudden tiring and began to analyse it. While I had been out running the course I'd set for myself my mind had been really active. I was thinking about the landmarks on the course, and mentally ticked off each one as I passed. I had been totally distracted from thinking about my body and its discomfort. I wondered if this was part of the key to running for long periods of time. My teachers at school had always said I was easily distracted. They seemed to think it was a weakness. They had obviously never been runners. I decided I must investigate this further.

After my ground-breaking first run I concluded that my shoes were pretty much beyond redemption and I would need new ones. The next day, in search of a bit of sole, I made a trip to my local sports store.

It wasn't really a sports shop as such; a better description would be sports barn. It was huge. I wandered in and out of the aisles in wonder. They had everything.

Against one wall I eventually found the footwear. Rows and rows of them. There were shoes for miles.

I knew I was in way over my head. When I was a kid I only had a few pairs of shoes and they were of a pretty basic design. Back then if you were going to run, you usually ran in sandshoes. Sandshoes were made of a hard rubbery sole with a canvas upper. They were white and in all respects very plain and simple. Not exactly the most comfortable pair of shoes you could find: after you had run a couple of miles the only thing they had going for them was that they just managed to dull some of the sharper stones you might tread on. And the canvas upper was a bit harsh on whatever part of the foot it came in contact with. It was advisable to wear socks to prevent blisters. At school when we got into our sports gear a low groan of anticipated agony told you someone had left their socks at home.

The angry pattern of gnarled rubber underneath the shoe looked impressive but in actual fact, unlike the soft rubber-soled shoes of today, was too damn hard to grip onto most surfaces. From time to time I would find out in our back garden an old sandshoe that had been living the quiet life, long forgotten in the tall grass and exposed to the weather for years. Invariably the canvas upper would have rotted away, leaving the hard sun-baked sole of the most durable sports shoe on the planet.

(Despite their shortcomings they were still a hit with schools and parents New Zealand-wide for two simple reasons. They were dirt cheap and there was nothing else available.)

As I stood surveying the array of shoes on offer I couldn't help thinking things had got a little out of control. There were shoes of every description for all manner of different sports, including one sport I had never heard of before called cross-training. It wasn't long before I decided I needed help.

A gaunt lad sporting a large, silly-looking name badge announcing him as 'Steve' appeared in my aisle. From the look of him Steve had been running since his feet first hit the floor. He was exactly what I imagined a white Kenyan distance runner would look like. He was quite tall and barely had an ounce of fat on him. I imagined him running mile after mile with a sadistic grin on his face and systematically destroying the will of other runners. Steve would be able to help me for sure.

He soon noticed me and wandered over.

'Can I help you, sir?'

'I'm looking for some running shoes.'

'What kind did you have in mind?'

'Oh I don't know really, just shoes to run in. Does it make much difference?'

As soon as I'd spoken I knew I had made a mistake. Steve, it turned out, knew a bit about shoes and with the zeal of a newly-converted Mormon he proceeded to impart his knowledge. I found it interesting at first. I'd never realized there was so much variety. There were shoes for the low-, medium- and high-mileage runner. Did I pronate, and if so, which way? Perhaps I required a neutral shoe? Was I going to run on the road or off-road? A bit of both perhaps?

I like listening to salespeople. There is something mesmerising about the sales pitch as they take you through all the possible options and product features. I find the technical jargon hardest to argue with and since I seldom know what the salesperson is talking about I just listen like a naughty schoolboy until the lecture is over. I usually end up buying whatever they recommend and can never remember the reason when challenged by my wife for spending too much.

I ended up walking to the checkout with a pretty impressive-looking pair of shoes. The soles looked as if they could grip on to a vertical ice wall. Steve thought they would be perfect for what I intended to do and he should know.

As I was leaving I asked him a parting question: 'You do a lot of running?'

'Nah,' he replied. 'I hate running.'

Chapter 7

Bringing It All Together

It was about this time that I met Graham. My wife and I watched with interest as our neighbours sold off a piece of land at the front of their property and a new house sprang up in a few short weeks. Soon after it was completed a family moved in and despite seeing them come and go almost daily nothing passed between us other than the occasional glance or a quick 'Hi'.

Graham seemed a nice-enough chap. He was about 5'8" with broad shoulders, and like me was probably carrying a little more weight around the waist than he wanted. He had medium-length greying hair and bore an unmistakable resemblance to a beardless Father Christmas. By a stunning coincidence, three of our other neighbours were also called Graham. To avoid confusion we privately referred to him as Graham Christmas. This differentiated him clearly from the others: Graham old, Graham four dogs and Graham melon-head, who gained their nicknames on account of their most notable feature.

One day when I was in a particularly neighbourly 'good will to all men' sort of mood I almost went over with a six-pack of beer to extend the hand of friendship but at the last moment my shyness got the better of me and I stayed home and drank the beer myself. I was soon a lot less shy but I'm not sure it would have been too wise to go anywhere.

It was quite a surprise, then, when one day, as I was staggering up our driveway after half an hour's run, Graham Christmas bravely strode the few metres between our properties, stuck out his hand and announced with a heavy accent, 'Gidday, mayt, I'm Garayum.'

'Excuse me?'

'I um Gar-ray-um, ya nayba.'

It turned out his name was Graham and he was my neighbour.

His accent was somewhere between Eastenders and Coronation Street and I found it difficult to understand everything he said. I listened politely. He seemed like a very nice chap and we ended up trying to communicate for about an hour.

From what I could work out Graham had spent his early years in England before coming out to New Zealand, later returning to England for several years, and finally making his home back in New Zealand. He loved the outdoors and told me that when his family had arrived in New Zealand he had been so captivated by the beauty of the wilderness he had spent much of his youth hiking in the hills.

He asked why I was running. It was the question I lived for. I proudly told him that I was planning to do the Coast to Coast and although I had only just started training, I was trying hard to attain a basic level of fitness.

Immediately he offered to help in any way he could and went on to say how he had always been interested in the Coast to Coast and had even gone to watch it. He asked me if I had organized my support crew to assist me during the race, and when I said no he immediately offered to fill the role, if I wanted.

He also told me he was a keen cyclist and before long was showing me the array of bikes he had in his garage. I was excited. Clearly I was on to a winner here. Not only was Graham willing to be my assistant during the event, but he almost certainly knew a lot more than I did about bikes. I couldn't help thinking it was a damn shame I hadn't made the effort to get to know him before I went off and purchased my own bike.

We walked over to my garage to have a look at the new bike. His smile faded the moment he saw it and I sensed from the way he said, 'I'm sorry but that's a piece of junk' that he had some reservations about it.

Graham's offer to be in my support crew made me realise I was going to need others too. I drew up a short list of friends and a couple of days later invited the two names at the top of the list to join Graham as support crew: Chris and Tony.

Chris was a long-time buddy of mine and a keen tramper. Not only was he very resourceful but his love of outdoor gadgetry would mean we would never be short on comfort. Chris always had the right gear for the right occasion. If you felt like a coffee in the middle of nowhere then

Chris was your man. He would rummage in his bag and a few minutes later he'd have a pot of hot water boiling over a violently hissing stove the size of a wallet. He had a better collection of Swiss army knives than the Swiss army.

Tony was more relaxed than anyone I knew. A tall, strapping surfer, he was seldom ruffled. He would be a calming influence in the heat of competition.

With the purchase of the necessary equipment, the choosing of my support crew and some tentative steps toward fitness, I felt I was now well on my way to the start line. But I also knew that it was the training in the months ahead that would make or break me. I had to move to the next level. It was time to put more of my focus on training.

It wasn't easy. I seemed to be very busy all the time. Without the luxury of independent wealth I still had to go to work everyday, spend time with my wife and children and do my share of the household chores. I ignored the garden. It could wait.

To start with I tried to do some kind of preparation for the race every day, even if it was only for a short time. Running was the easiest to organise: I could just get into my gear and pop off for 20 or 30 minutes at the drop of a hat.

Cycling wasn't too bad either. I got into my cycling gear, went out to the garage, pumped up the tyres and did a quick check over the bike, before wobbling off down the driveway.

Kayaking required the most effort. I had to haul my kayak out of the garage and fight it on to the car. At five and a half metres long it was difficult to manoeuvre. I was always banging it into things and it's a wonder it ever got to the river in one piece. After the kayak was tethered on I had to round up the spray skirt, lifejacket, paddle, a cap, find my kayak shoes and get into my kayaking clothes. I then drove the 300 metres from my house to the river.

At first I felt bad driving such a short distance to the river. Then one day my wife had taken the car and I had to walk to and from the river lugging all my kayak gear. It was a huge struggle to manhandle the boat and all the gear to the river but it was far worse on the way home. After an hour's kayaking all the gear was waterlogged and much heavier and the walk seemed twice as far. I was shattered when I finally made it home, and never felt guilty taking the car again.

I continued to gather all the information I could about the race and training disciplines. I read every book and magazine I could about kayaking, biking, running and fitness. I found that a little bit of knowledge could be dangerous. Reading so many different opinions can be confusing and I had a new theory every week. One week I would read about the benefits of hill training and I'd spend every spare minute training in the hills. The next week I'd read about the importance of speed work and I'd flog myself senseless doing sprints and repetitions. It was hell on my body. In fact some weeks I'd end up having to take a few days off training to recover from my latest theory.

One useful thing I did learn from all my reading was to try experimenting with different types of food while training. I tried a number of nutrition bars and gels before I settled on bananas, a sugary gel I liked the taste of, and a type of food bar. These became my exercise sustenance.

While the act of getting each of these energy sources from the packaging to my mouth varied in difficulty for me, it was the gel that proved most difficult to master. It came in plastic sachets that were almost impossible to open, so that sometimes I'd end up in a vicious fight with the sachet as I tried to rip it open with my teeth, mid-way through whatever was that day's training session. When it did open, more often than not I ended up with most of the contents on my clothes and hands and very little in my mouth. The gel itself was very sticky and after fumbling through a few of them I would find my hands sticking to everything I came in contact with. The plastic sachets were forever turning up stuck to various items of my running gear. My wife was constantly finding them in the washing machine. Once one dropped to the floor in the shower as I washed my hair.

Despite all this I persisted with them for one simple reason: they worked. Once when I'd been out running for an hour or so I was almost completely spent, only to be completely revived in a matter of minutes by a sachet of gel and a couple of mouthfuls of water. After I'd discovered this I never set out on a run of over thirty minutes without one in my running bag.

As I got stronger and fitter I began to go on the odd adventure.

One day Graham and I decided to ride from home to a small town called Oxford, about 60 kilometres away. We each carried two water bottles on our bikes and a camelback drinking system with two litres of water on our backs. We set off early one Saturday morning full of high spirits and excited about the day ahead. Graham was feeling especially exuberant and set off at a cracking pace up the road. Realising it was going to be a long ride I let him go and soon he was a hundred metres ahead. We had gone no more than about a kilometre when I saw the strangest sight. Up ahead of me and without any warning whatsoever, Graham did a forward somersault over the handlebars of his bike and hit the ground, landing on his back. As he did so there was a muffled explosion that echoed down the road.

I rode up to him, incredulous. He was back on his feet and standing beside his bike with a look of complete bewilderment on his face.

'What the hell happened?' I asked.

'I don't know,' he said. 'One second I was looking around to see where you were and the next I was on the ground.'

'Are you hurt?' I asked, completely puzzled.

'I don't think so but could you take a look at my back? It feels wet. I must be bleeding.'

He turned around to reveal no blood whatsoever.

'It's only water!' I exclaimed, and then it dawned on me. The crash, the explosion, the water. I started laughing.

Graham looked at me in disgust. 'Well thanks a bloody lot.'

I could barely contain myself. 'You silly tit. You must have turned your handlebars when you looked around to see where I was. You locked up the front wheel. The explosion was your camelback, that's where all the water's come from.'

Graham surveyed his bike then took off his now-flattened camelback and as he did so a sheepish smile began to creep across his face.

'Bugger,' was all he said.

He picked up his bike and we carried on out to Oxford and back. I'm not sure how long it took us but we had a great day. One thing was for certain though: Graham was a darn sight more careful when looking behind after that.

* * *

A few weeks later, Don invited Sharon and me on a kayak trip down the lower reaches of the Waimakariri River. About an hour or so down-river we ran out of things to talk about and the dreary discomfort of the long-distance kayaker began to descend on the three of us. Don led, with Sharon some 20 metres behind him, while I hung back the same distance behind her.

Not long after, we came to a fork in the river. I was somewhat surprised when Don took the right fork and Sharon took the left. Because he was my kayaking mentor I followed Don to the right. The braid took us further and further to the right and the surroundings were soon quite different from the middle of the river plain, with its featureless gravel and stark vista. Willow trees and thick scrub meant Sharon was soon out of sight altogether.

I followed along behind Don at a respectable distance until I noticed a sudden change in his behaviour. As I watched he stopped paddling and half turned his head as if listening to something. He sat up alert and then suddenly started paddling like a madman for the left-hand bank. I watched in surprise as he seemed to change his mind, then he stopped, braced himself against some unseen force and promptly dropped out of sight.

I immediately knew what had happened.

'Oh my God, he's gone over a weir … sideways.' In no time I was faced with the same predicament.

In the next instant I came of age as a kayaker. I saw a steep drop of two metres. I saw Don at the bottom, shaken but still upright. I saw Sharon across the turbulent pool at the bottom, looking on in horror. I saw the willow trees at the end of the pool waiting to trap and drown me and I saw what I had to do.

I straightened up to go head-on. There was no way I was going to try it sideways. I steeled myself and charged over the drop.

The bottom of my boat screeched in protest as the concrete weir clawed at it in passing. I shot past the nose of Don's kayak, a mere whisker from smashing it in half, and crashed into the pool at the foot of the weir. The boat wobbled violently as it fell but eventually I regained control. The three of us sat shaking as Sharon told us of her horror upon seeing the weir and realising she had no time to warn us. It was a lucky escape.

It was not my last. On another day, as I was driving home from a successful afternoon's kayaking on a nearby river, I noticed the wind coming up. I was just beginning to wonder if my kayak would stay on the racks when the whole lot flew off the top of the car and disappeared. I screeched to a halt, turned around and drove back, expecting to find my expensive kayak in a thousand pieces. It wasn't. At a hundred kilometres an hour, it had flown off the car, ripping the roof racks off with it, landed upright on the racks, skidded through an open farm gate and two metres beyond it, and somehow remained in one piece. It was a true miracle in every sense. Either of the gateposts could have broken the kayak in half. I found a couple of scratches near the rudder but that was it.

As I trained and read and listened and learnt the days turned into weeks and the weeks to months. The weather began to improve and with it so did my strength and stamina and my prospects of completing this huge undertaking I had started months before. As spring came and was soon replaced by summer my confidence began to build. I felt different. I felt stronger, fitter and more alive.

I wanted more.

I increased my efforts and tried to train every day. The cool clear mornings and pleasant mild evenings became my companions as I covered the city by foot, bike and kayak. Work finished, Christmas and holidays came and went and January's summer heat blew into February and my training wound down and finally stopped. I had been told to rest for the week leading up to the race. I ate a lot and slept and rested. The days dragged by. Hour by hour, minute by minute, time slowed and began to crawl. I began to feel restless, edgy, agitated. I was ready and knew it.

I craved exercise like a strung-out addict but knew I had to hold out. I had to arrive at race day literally fit to bust, a coiled spring, ready to unleash myself. I had to be desperate to start. By the time the lads and I packed the cars and headed for Kumara I was there.

Chapter 8

Race Day

On the morning of the race I woke at 4am. I didn't need to be awake for another hour but figured I was lucky to get any sleep at all considering how long I had been preparing for this day. As soon as I was aware of where I was my heart started racing with excitement and nervousness. I stayed in bed, trying to relax. I knew that the time for action would arrive soon enough and didn't want to start to soon the preparation that would see me focused and nervous until the race started and I could finally release the energy that had been building for days.

The motel was quiet. We had arrived late the previous evening after a very entertaining briefing at the Kumara town hall. Robin Judkins had been in a jovial mood as he went over the race details. He joked and jested with whoever caught his attention. When a woman rose to leave for the toilet he pounced: 'Boring you, am I?' The crowd erupted in laughter. No one was spared: a Welsh film crew fussing over their camera gear were teased mercilessly every time they moved – 'Oh, what is it now?' The crowd loved every minute. This was the Judkins they had heard about.

He gleefully told tales of worried competitors phoning and asking inane questions about minute details of the race. 'What do I do with my bike at the end of the bike section?' 'Where can I get food at Klondyke corner?' He chastised the worriers, often by name, and surfed the waves of laughter wherever they broke.

Soon it came time to explain the safety details and Judkins gradually became serious. He started quietly reading through the safety rules one by one but the longer he went on the louder he got. It was as if with every rule he read he became more aware of the weight of his responsibilities until he was shouting over the microphone as he reminded all cyclists to stay on the left-hand side of the road at all times.

The delivery of his warnings however was so forceful it was hard to keep a straight face. I noticed spontaneous smiling and nervous giggling. Everyone knew the message was serious but the delivery was so over the top. I myself had a terrible time fighting an almost overwhelming hysterical laugh that drove its way up from my lungs as he boomed out the last of the safety instructions. It had been a hell of a show.

As I lay there in bed I surveyed the bland white walls of my room and my mind returned to the day ahead. I wanted to think about anything but the race, however, my mind kept coming back to it. I needed a distraction.

I reached for the race handbook and lay there scanning all the names and occupations of my fellow competitors. Soon I was engrossed.

Of course there was the usual array of conventional occupations: doctors, lawyers, accountants, painters, cooks, fishermen and the like, but there was also a smattering of the interesting and unusual. One person had listed his occupation as a pot washer, another was a fat trader. I wondered what exactly a microbiology manager might do for a living. There was a person listed as a leather technician, another as a gum digger; a trucker, a bum and there were two ministers of religion. There was also a 'river-bed inspector' listed but I assumed the title had more to do with how he might be travelling the river during the kayak section than anything else.

Each competitor had been asked to supply a brief background of 10 words or less for the race programme. Judging by some of the comments you'd be forgiven for thinking that New Zealanders are a strange lot. One fellow stated he was the 'World record holder in sperm donation'. Another's read, 'Just plain stupid'. My favourite simply stated, 'My carcass is a temple, such punishment will bring purity'. Everyone had a reason, or an excuse, for taking on this huge challenge.

However, after 15 minutes of reading I was bored and starting to get nervous again. I decided to have a shave. Having a shower crossed my mind but I had already learnt the painful way that washing under my arms and in certain other places had the effect of removing enough of the skin's natural oils to cause serious chafing during exercise.

After shaving I decided to eat. I had a quick breakfast of toast and tea and a small bowl of peaches. It was 5am and time to wake up the crew.

Tony went for the shower, Graham went for breakfast and Chris stayed in bed pretending that none of us existed.

I went outside for a look around. It was still dark and quite brisk. I could see plenty of stars. It was going to be a fine day. Other units in the motel were coming to life. A light went on. I could hear hushed voices from the next block and a motor idling quietly. Race day was here. I let the nerves start to play in my stomach: it wouldn't be too long now.

Back inside, the boys were packing up. Chris had had one of his legendary 60-second cold showers and was half-dressed and chewing on some breakfast.

We finished packing and briefly went over the plans for the day before doing a quick check of the bike tyres and making sure the kayak was still secured to racks on the car roof.

With that we set off for the bike racks, where I would set up my trusty steed, then walk back the 2.8 kilometres to the beach to await the start.

We arrived at the bike racks to find what looked like chaos. There were people, cars and bikes everywhere. But as I watched I began to see the patterns. The crowds converged from all directions but once the cycles were in the racks the group split. The competitors began their nervous trek west toward the beach and the support crews headed east to the next transition point 55 kilometres away.

Chris stopped beside the bike stand and I racked my bike and fussed around it checking the tyre pressure and making sure it was in an easy gear to start cycling. I was reluctant to leave it and head for the beach but soon I had no choice as a marshal came along and scurried Chris into his car and got him moving. With a cheery 'Good luck' he was gone and there was nothing for me to do but head for the beach.

In the pre-dawn chill I walked briskly to keep warm, passing a long line of cars with people waiting for their opportunity to stop and rack their bikes. In every car faces peered out nervously as they sought the assigned spot for their bike. Soon I had passed them all and found myself walking in loose association with a large number of other competitors rustling their way down the road toward the beach. The rustling came from the sound of plastic rubbish bags that many of my fellow competitors wore as protection against the cold. I was quite cold now and wished I had one too.

The call of nature was proving very strong for many and on the way to the beach each of the portable toilets, spaced every few hundred metres, had a waiting throng. There is something distinctly unsavoury about portable toilets. To me they are the western equivalent of open sewers. I never feel comfortable being around them. For one thing, I can't understand why you would make a receptacle the colour of an emergency beacon for something so private. When a bright orange door opens it catches the eye of people hundreds of metres away. I don't know about you but when I emerge from a public toilet I would prefer that the world didn't know.

From time to time small groups of men rejoicing in the fact that they were liberated at least half the time from the need to enter these smelly little dens were happily urinating at the side of the road. I joined one such group and for a moment the banter made me forget my pre-race nerves. Other urinators came and went and the joking continued, fuelled by a constant supply of new members. I would have stayed longer but we all knew the unwritten rules: you did your business and moved on, anything else was unacceptable.

Standing on the small embankment that overlooked the beach I was greeted with an impressive sight. Over the water the sky was lightening with the approaching dawn, while in the foreground big waves crashed onto the steep West Coast beach, which was awash with humanity. Hundreds of athletes were spread out over the beach in various stages of readiness, going through an array of pre-race rituals. Some were stretching, others chatting in small groups. Some ran this way and that. More than a few were down at the water's edge, where they sought to touch the cool waters of the Tasman Sea, with the hope and expectation that tomorrow they would do the same, on the other side of the country, in the Pacific Ocean.

To the south in the distance I could see clearly the pyramid of Aoraki Mount Cook rising out of the Southern Alps – at 3,754 metres New Zealand's tallest.

I strode purposefully on to the beach and headed for the water. I reached the edge, waited for a wave, and then deftly touched the wash as it shot up the beach. As I stood there rejoicing in the moment a man just in front of me was surprised by the next wave. It surged forward and nearly knocked him off his feet. He got wet up to his knees and clambered up the beach looking sheepish. No one could say he hadn't touched the Tasman Sea.

I wandered around exchanging nervous grimaces with other competitors until I remembered I wanted to take a memento back to my family. I stooped and chose three small pebbles from the beach, one for my wife and one each for the children. I would carry them from coast to coast.

Maybe it was the lack of sleep, maybe it was the excitement of the day or maybe it was thoughts of family and what it had taken for me to get to this point in my life but for a moment emotion almost overcame me.

I stood up quickly. Damn dust – always getting in my eyes.

I had nowhere else to put the pebbles so I popped them into the small food pocket on the back of the cycle top I was wearing. Already in the pocket were a couple of flattened sandwiches and some nuts and pieces of dried fruit, fuel for the journey.

Just when I was beginning to wonder when we might be starting Robin Judkins appeared on the embankment above the beach and the competitors began to creep forward to take up their start positions. Megaphone in one hand, and air horn in the other, Judkins waved us all back until we were at the water's edge. He garbled something about great weather, having a good day and looking out for each other, before he raised the horn. A mournful note blared out across the beach and we all charged forward. Away at last.

I ran faster than I should have for the embankment in front of me. As I wondered how to get up it others, picking their way between the rocks, beat me up. I followed them onto the gravel road that lead away from the beach. On the road I continued running hard as the excitement took hold, but before long it struck me that if I kept up this pace I would be a wreck in about another three minutes. I eased up and almost immediately it seemed like the whole world began to pass me. I fought the urge to speed up again, especially when the oldest and most wrinkly man in the world struggled past with a grin from ear to ear, closely followed by a colossus of a man who would have been at least twice my weight. He defied every law of running known to man yet here he was carrying his considerable bulk toward a bike that I assumed would be something like a Harley-Davidson with the motor ripped out.

Kumara beach. Robin Judkins, the ringmaster, poses for the media before doing what he does best: launching a thousand competitors off on the adventure of their lives. Michael Jacques

Soon we began to run up a small incline. As the race stretched out before me I marvelled that some runners had got so far ahead so quickly. I began to feel the incline, but not as much as some others. I caught up with Mr Wrinkly. The old guy was breathing hard and had slowed considerably but he still wore a manic grin like some evil clown. I passed Mr Colossus near the top of the incline. His breathing was so hard and loud it couldn't be healthy. I hoped he wasn't going to drop dead.

Once at the top of the incline I settled into an easy rhythm and began to feel quite comfortable and more aware of the surroundings. I noticed there were a few spectators at the side of the road. Presumably they lived in the one or two houses that lined the road and obviously they were keen to catch a glimpse of the yearly circus as it passed by. Some cheered while others just smiled at the masses as they huffed and puffed their way up the road. We passed one house where a couple were sitting on their deck in armchairs sipping coffee. The man was puffing on a half-smoked cigarette and I couldn't help thinking that would have been me a few years ago – at seven in the morning it would probably have been my second cigarette.

As I ran on for what seemed a long time I was starting to wonder where the transition point had got to. Perhaps someone had collected all the bikes and moved them a few extra kilometres down the road. They were nowhere to be seen. But not long after, the crowd of runners ahead of me parted and suddenly I saw them. As I reached the first bikes I noticed the numbers were in the early three hundreds so I kept running, looking for the start of the three hundreds in search of 328.

I located my bike and pulled it out of the rack. Everything looked in order. As others around me struggled to take off running shoes and replace them with cycling shoes I mounted my bike and wobbled off. As I took care to get my feet into the cages I must have wobbled into the path of another cyclist because someone whizzed by and snarled, 'Keep your line.' I took this to mean that wobbling around was not helpful to other riders and so I tried to go straight.

As I set out on the long, straight road a loose bunch began to form around me. By the time we had been going for no more than five minutes we were 50 cyclists. I felt a bit nervous with so many other riders in such close proximity but no one did anything unexpected and soon I was feeling more confident. I wasn't breathing too hard and physically felt quite comfortable. It wasn't long before I was positively enjoying myself.

I made sure to watch the rear wheel of the cyclist immediately in front of me and keep a couple of feet back. Every now and then I would look ahead past the front of my bunch and further up the road and I could see at least two other bunches with approximately the same number of cyclists working away together.

The pace was quite good. The bunch was ticking along at around 35 kilometres per hour and I was surprised at how easily I could maintain this speed when on my own in training I had found it difficult to get beyond about 30 kilometres per hour. The answer came shortly afterward when I pulled over to one side of the bunch and momentarily faced the force of the wind on my own. Without the shelter of the bunch a much harder effort was required. I sidled my way back into the safety of the pack. I marvelled at the strength of the riders at the front of the bunch as they took turns bearing the full brunt of the wind for anywhere from 20 seconds to a minute or so before peeling out to the side and drifting back to the shelter of the bunch. Here they would rest a while before creeping back up to the front for another turn. Little was said but there was a lot of exchange. The riders seemed to communicate with subtle hand signals. If someone took a long turn at the front it seemed to be appreciated.

We were like a flock of geese flying in formation, though instead of honking support and encouragement we nodded at each other. And just like a flock of geese the strongest were up the front sharing the work while down the back the freeloaders, including myself, were enjoying the benefits of their not inconsiderable labours.

We passed through the small township of Kumara, with its simple array of shops and houses, to the cheers and applause of some of the locals. It was a great feeling to be cheered. I tried to think back to when I had last been even the partial recipient of any cheering. The only recent occasion I could remember was when a friend and I were clapped wildly as we jogged past a group waiting for a bus outside a mental hospital.

Soon after leaving the township we began a gradual ascent of a small hill. The bunch slowed considerably and everyone had to work, even those at the back. We made our way to the top of the rise and I steeled myself for what was to come. We were about to make a seven-kilometre

Keep your line! Wobbling off from the bike stands into the early morning sunlight, after a quick 2.8km run up from Kumara Beach. Paul's Camera Shop

descent, during which we would reach speeds of around 75 kilometres per hour – and do so in close proximity to each other. The road descended in a number of stages. First there was a steep descent, followed by a short plateau about a hundred metres in length. Then there were more descents of varying lengths each punctuated with a short plateau and a moment's respite before another headlong rush down the hill.

Surrounded by a native bush reserve of rare beauty, this short section of the road concerned me more than any other. I knew from books and magazine articles I had read and from a variety of witnesses that over the years there had been some hideous accidents on this section. It only took one rider to touch the wheel of another and the resulting crash could bring down a dozen others. Those following would have little or no time to react. By the time you realised that the sickening horror unravelling in slow motion right in front of you was going to include you it was too late. In a matter of seconds you would be flying through the air for your own date with the road.

We roared down the first part of the descent without incident. I stayed out on the left-hand side of the bunch so if anything happened I'd have a chance to land on grass and ferns rather than road. My fingers hovered over the brakes. I had been told that the best way to react to anything untoward happening ahead of me was to gently squeeze the brakes, rather than jam them full-on, potentially causing a pile-up behind.

I kept this in mind as we roared down the next section. I 'held my line' and got into a lower, more aerodynamic position and was quite surprised to find myself gaining rather quickly on the riders just in front of me. A few gentle taps on the brakes restored a safe distance. I was enjoying myself and my confidence grew.

We were getting up to speeds of around 70 kilometres per hour during the steeper downhill sections, but on the short plateaus the bunch would close up slightly and the speed would drop to around 40 kilometres per hour. By the time we had reached the last long, steep and fast section I was having so much fun that I carefully made my way out to the right flank of the bunch and got into the most aerodynamic tuck I could. I bent my knees in close together and got my head down so low that my chin was almost on the handlebar stem. It felt rather uncomfortable but boy did I start to get some momentum! I gained on the cyclists in front of me at an alarming rate but because I had positioned myself on the outside of the bunch I was able to come up behind them in their slipstream, then scoot by quickly and safely.

Soon I worked my way right up to very near the front of the bunch. As we came to the bottom of the hill and our speed dropped to a more sedate 35 kilometres per hour I realised I was sitting about five behind the lead rider. As we hissed along I looked around at the lean and hungry riders around me. Hunched low on their machines, they glanced dispassionately at me. I had done nothing.

I knew I wouldn't last long but now that I was here I decided to stay long enough to do my bit. As the riders did their stint at the front and peeled off I steeled myself for my turn. Soon I was third in line, then second and suddenly my turn had arrived. As the rider in front peeled off I alone felt the full force of the wind. It was exhilarating to be leading and to know that the whole bunch was feeding off my work.

At the same time, looking up the road with no one in front of me was strange. I could have been alone. I felt naked and exposed.

After 30 seconds I was beginning to tire. I suspected the secret to longevity at the front of the bunch was to take it in short turns but also knew I probably wasn't going to do this again so I held on. I kept my speed at an even 35 kilometres per hour but soon had to work harder to keep it there. My leg muscles started to hurt. My breathing began to labour. Beads of sweat rolled out from under my helmet, down my forehead and into my eyes. I knew my time was up.

After one minute and 10 seconds leading the bunch I peeled away. I felt almost instant relief. Another rider was now at the front, exposed. The train moved on. As the engine room came past one of them nodded. I nodded back as casually as I could.

I faded further and further until I found shelter near the back of the bunch. I was sweating profusely and felt ragged. Other cyclists relaxing at the back of the bunch looked at me with curious stares. I couldn't have cared less. I had led the bunch.

Chapter 9

Life on the Road

We entered a long straight and I could see two potential problems: in the distance a longish climb, and part-way up that climb, another bunch of riders.

It was, since shortly after the start, the first time I had seen anyone ahead of us. I was not the only one to notice them. Quickly the pace of our bunch increased to around 39 kilometres per hour; it seemed that the chase was on. I was forced to work harder just to stay on the wheel of the riders in front. Whereas before we had moved forward three or four abreast, as the pace increased we were down to two abreast and, for a short time, single file.

The pace eased somewhat as we hit the lower section of the long, gradual climb, but back in the tail of the bunch the effect of the extra effort was being felt. All around me riders were breathing heavily and I wasn't surprised to look over my shoulder and see we had lost four members. For them there would be little hope of regaining the bunch. We were now consistently moving at around 37 kilometres per hour on the flat – a speed few cyclists could manage on their own for long periods.

However, when I looked back a few minutes later I saw a strange sight. The four who had dropped off our bunch had become five. I wondered if I had missed one the last time I had looked but didn't think so. The next time I looked back a lone figure had left the other four of the group and made out on his own. He was after us!

I couldn't believe it. An individual was chasing our bunch – and gaining – at a time when we were ourselves chasing another bunch! He must be a hell of a cyclist, I thought to myself.

For the next while I didn't have occasion to look back. My bunch was now getting close to the bunch in front and I had to concentrate as the speed ebbed and flowed. At times while in single file a rider might start to lose touch with the rider in front of them. This caused a minor panic for those of us behind as we were forced to pass this rider with a short burst of effort to re-connect to the main bunch. The stakes were high. Fail and we would be cast adrift for a long slow ride and, like the four we had left behind earlier, only a small number to share the work.

Mercifully our bunch finally caught the bunch in front. Most of us heaved a collective sigh of relief and rested for a while before starting to integrate with the other group. However, the engine room of our bunch almost immediately began to drift forward to the front of the new combined bunch and despite their presence the pace of the new combined bunch did not quicken as I thought it might. It seemed they had proved themselves and were happy to sit back a bit and enjoy the ride, at least for a while.

This suited me fine. I stayed down the back of the bunch, among the last ten or so riders, recovering from my exertions.

A little later I happened to glance behind me. I was shocked to see the rider who had apparently been chasing our bunch was now only a few metres away and about to join us. I immediately recognised him. It was Mr Colossus, the huge man who had passed me in the short run up from the beach but whom I had caught up with a few minutes later. He certainly didn't look to be suffering now, as he had appeared to be during the run. I guessed that the answer lay in the fact that his thighs were as big as tree trunks – no use for running but exactly what you needed to be a powerful cyclist.

He smiled as he joined us at the back of the bunch where he could shelter behind the other riders. If he was tired from his solo effort to catch up with us he didn't show it. He simply sat up and began to refuel. From behind his back he produced a banana which he quickly ate and replaced with another. In fact over the next few minutes he devoured the second banana, two sandwiches, a fruit bar and some biscuits. He washed this down with about a litre of water before burping loudly and cycling off toward the front of the bunch. I half expected to see a small fridge strapped to his back as he passed. He did however have the next best thing, in the form of three large and bulging pockets on his cycle top that I assumed contained more sustenance (possibly even whole chickens) for the road ahead.

I was feeling a lot better now that the pace had become more manageable. I was not the only one. Others around me seemed to be enjoying the journey as well and soon the hiss of cycles was joined by the buzz of conversation. We talked about the speed of the downhill, the pace of the chase, the size of the bunch and all things cycling.

I met other New Zealanders. Mark from Auckland, Jed from Invercargill and Jane from Nelson. I also met Frank from Wichita, Kansas and Chris from Scotland. It was a bit like the United Nations.

With conversation and the easy pace everyone began to relax. The zealots at the front of the bunch seemed to be in no hurry to rev things up and once this was obvious we all took the opportunity to take on food and water.

I had carefully attempted to have a drink from my water bottle a couple of times with only minimal success. Taking the bottle meant leaving only one hand on the handlebars. I felt relatively comfortable steering with one hand but getting the bottle in the first place required reaching down to where it was secured in its cage while steering the bike and watching the rider in front of me so as not to collide. It was the combination of performing all three of these tasks simultaneously that made the act so potentially treacherous.

The drink bottle is secured close to the front wheel, so if when I reached down for it I happened to overshoot, I might find when I brought my hand back up that I was short a few fingers. As unlikely as it might sound, this is not impossible. I read recently that in the Tour de France cycle race one rider managed to sever the end of one finger while adjusting part of his speedometer. I wondered how he explained that to his colleagues. He had to be right up there with the guy I once read about who kept a loaded pistol beside his bed and shot his ear off when the phone rang one night.

After a few dummy runs I managed to get hold of the bottle, take a couple of gulps of water and successfully replace it. Replacing the bottle was more difficult than I thought it would be but I managed it on my third attempt. Others clearly were not so successful.

I was alarmed by sudden shouting and animated arm waving before I narrowly missed hitting a water bottle that had been dropped by a rider in front. There was some heated conversation further up the bunch but the only word I recognised was 'shithead'.

As if this episode was the signal for others to start accidentally offloading gear, next we were all swerving to avoid a small pump, followed a few minutes later by another water bottle, this time still attached to the cage that was supposed to secure it to the owner's bike. Soon after I got a hell of a fright to see what I initially thought was a small animal bouncing around between the bikes after being hit by successive riders. It turned out to be a spare tube.

Next to start appearing on the road surface was various kinds of food. Bananas seemed to be a favourite. Peeling a banana with one hand while in the middle of a bunch of cyclists at 35 kilometres per hour is not easy.

I watched one chap take some time to examine his banana from all angles before taking an unceremonious chunk (skin and all) out of the side of it. He then spat out the mouthful and, not unlike a wild dog or frenzied shark, returned to bite the banana and shake his head in an attempt to free the part he intended to eat.

Food bars were worse. Not only were they hell to open but they cost about $5 each. Dropping them was expensive. The shark/dog frenzy technique was wholly unsuccessful with most food bars and could end in the cyclist eating the foil packaging as well as the bar owing to a tendency for the two to stick together.

I noticed, however, that one of the two women in our bunch had mastered the food-unwrapping problem with simple logic. Prior to the race she had opened the bars, squashed them up into little balls and used their own stickiness to attach them to the handlebars of her bike. They looked like little brown blobs of Blu-tack. She would simply take a piece as she required it. Later I saw her pull out a piece of banana from the back of her cycle top. It had been pre cut into a manageable bite size and the skin had been sliced to improve access. With one hand she deftly skinned the banana and ate it without so much as a wobble. She had obviously put more thought into the ride/eat problem than many of us.

My own endeavours to eat were successful apart from the fact that some idiot had put three small pebbles into the pouch that contained my sandwiches and I nearly cracked a tooth when I bit into one of them.

Now that the period of refuelling was over the bunch got back to the serious business of riding and the pace began to quicken. I strained to look up the road, trying to ascertain the reason for the rush but there was nothing to see. The pace stayed high for a few minutes and then just as quickly settled down again and the bunch returned to its general cruising shape of three and four abreast at a speed of around 33 kilometres per hour.

Considering all the food and bits and pieces of cycling paraphernalia our bunch had dropped, it was a miracle that no one had either hit something and come off or collided with another rider, but I had the feeling that the bunch was a little too relaxed. Since the feeding frenzy I had begun to notice there were more close shaves. Someone would suddenly become aware that their front wheel was almost touching the back wheel of the rider in front of them and they would sometimes be forced to take evasive action. When tires did touch there would be a small commotion followed by the pungent smell of burning rubber. On occasion angry words were exchanged.

With each close shave I began to feel less safe cycling at the rear of the bunch. I had just made up my mind to join the more experienced riders toward the front of the bunch when in front of me one rider moved into the path of another. In the resulting commotion brakes squealed, tyres burned, tempers flared. I realised that had there been a crash I would have been unable to avoid it. I carefully dropped back further toward the rear and then when I had clear space I worked my way around the right flank, up to the front ten or so riders, and slotted into the pack again. I then worked my way over to the left of the bunch, where I felt more comfortable, and looked around.

The front of the bunch was quite different from the back. For a start, every time any obstacle appeared ahead on the road the riders in front would point at it and call a warning. 'Possum' came the cry when a dead opossum in the middle of the lane confronted the leaders and others behind repeated the warning. This never happened at the back of the bunch. All we would hear was, 'Shit, look out!' and cyclists would be violently swerving all over the place. At the front the call would be 'One lane bridge, close up,' and we would close up and go through comfortably. At the back you sensed a commotion ahead then suddenly the approach to the bridge appeared and five cyclists tried desperately to cram into a space that might comfortably fit three. At the front of the bunch any movement by a rider was telegraphed with hand signals and if necessary a polite apology. At the back of the bunch you might be talking to someone and some idiot would come up from behind and try to cycle through the impossibly narrow gap between the two of you. It was scary stuff.

I liked it at the front. The pace was manageable for the present and there was a more experienced and better class of rider. It felt safe.

I soon found myself chatting amicably to a doctor on one side and a plumber on the other. The doctor had done the race a number of times and said he never cycled down the back of a bunch because he considered it too dangerous. I told him that that was precisely why I had come to the front of the bunch and we smiled at each other smugly.

I turned back to talk to the plumber when suddenly I heard someone ahead say 'Oh no' and I turned back to see that the rider in front of the doctor had overshot and hit the wheel of the rider in front of him. I watched in horror as the rider fought to control the front wheel of his bike. In what seemed like slow motion his weight started to fall to the left and further into the wheel of the rider in front until he violently jerked his handlebars to the right, causing a wild swerve across in that direction that corrected him enough to remain upright. The flow-on effect of his action, however, saw the doctor beside me have the front wheel of his bike suddenly smashed sidewards and with a sickening thud he hit the ground and was gone.

Around me conversation stopped. The only sound was the quiet hum of cycles. No one said a word.

I felt ill. The poor bastard. I knew he must have brought down other riders but because it had all happened behind me I had hardly heard a thing.

The imagined aftermath played heavily on my mind. I could picture the clash of metal and bodies as they struck the harsh road surface. This would be followed by the groans of the injured and the cursing of those with damaged bikes, their frustration mounting as they struggled to untangle themselves while watching the bunch disappear up the road. For them it was still a race but for those more seriously hurt their hopes of completing the journey on the back of a whole year's training and sacrifice were over.

The crash had a sobering effect on the bunch. The pace dropped ever so slightly and you could almost feel the increase in concentration. Slowly the chatter of conversation began to return, but it was different now. Riders spoke quietly, in almost hushed tones as if waiting for the family of the deceased to leave the church at a funeral.

There was also a notable increase in tension. Riders became even more communicative and any movement around the bunch was preceded by an apology from the moving rider, if not a detailed explanation as to why and how they intended to move so there would be no catastrophic mix-ups. If someone had produced a permit to say they had approval to move over two spaces I wouldn't have been surprised.

Just how much tension had built was soon obvious. The appearance of two trucks on the horizon sent shock waves through the bunch. I'd thought the level of agitation and concern when a water bottle was dropped was a bit over the top but it paled in comparison to the outright panic that spread through the group as the trucks approached. Riders couldn't get out of the way fast enough and in no time the bunch flattened itself against the left-hand verge. We glared at the drivers as the two farm trucks drove by but they barely noticed us. It was as if they were used to seeing large groups of brightly-attired cyclists snaking up the road every day.

I wondered if their indifference to us was purely a matter of the degree of the threat. Whereas to us they were the metallic equivalent of the horsemen of the apocalypse and had to be avoided at all costs, to them we might as well have been a swarm of bugs. You just drive through them and wipe them off.

Judkins had said at the race briefing the night before that he had secured a partial road closure. This meant that for all intents and purposes the road was closed but even so he warned us to stay to the left. This was because some people didn't give a damn about road closures and if they wanted to visit their six-fingered relatives down the road they would and to hell with any cyclists that got in the way.

This attitude was more than obvious in our next visitor. The bunch was still a bit edgy after the appearance of the trucks when a car started to come up from behind us. Even before I saw it I knew that it was a big car. It rumbled ominously. I glanced back at it. Its heavily chromed front seemed to take up half the road. At the top of the chrome began a huge blue bonnet, which eased into a gently sloping windscreen.

I was surprised to see a woman driving. She had what appeared to be another woman with her in the front and in the back sat two very aggressive-looking dogs. The dogs were up at the open window with their tongues hanging out and their eyes fixed on us as if they were being driven past a smorgasbord.

The car rumbled up beside the last few members of the bunch and it began to look very much as if the driver was probing for a way through. There was barely enough room to pass but that was not going to stop her.

What followed was the longest and most dangerous overtaking manoeuvre I have ever seen. The driver crossed over the centre line and then, instead of increasing speed and passing us quickly, she kept pace with us and ever so slowly began to crawl past. I found this tremendously unnerving. Having this huge machine rumbling alongside us was like having someone drive a motor-mower within two inches of your head: it probably won't kill you but it sure as hell doesn't feel comfortable.

I wasn't the only one who felt vulnerable. A murmur of concern began to ripple through the bunch. Soon the straight section of road we were on began to run out and she was still on the wrong side of the road. Ahead the road disappeared around a bend. It dawned on me that anyone else who might have ignored the road closure and be coming toward us around the next bend was going to have two choices. They could either run head-on into a few tonnes of American steel or they could veer into the nice soft juicy cyclists in the other lane. I knew which choice I would make.

As we approached the bend it became obvious that everyone else had come to the same conclusion and the murmur of concern became a tirade of abuse. Ordinarily I never yell abuse at anyone, but under the influence of the mixture of fear, anger and righteous indignation of the mob I joined in with full voice.

Although the driver probably couldn't decipher a word that was said the noise and alarm from the bunch immediately had the desired effect. The car's deep rumble became suddenly more urgent and the great hulk lurched forward, finally passing the front of the bunch before careering around the bend.

The group breathed a collective sigh of relief. And rolled on.

We soon began a long but slight ascent up to the tiny settlement of

One of the big cycle bunches in cruise mode during the 55-kilometre ride to the first transition station at Aickens Corner. Note how the riders toward the rear have spread to both sides of the road. Michael Jacques

Jacksons. The most prominent feature of the town is the old tavern. Built in the early 1860s, Jackson's Tavern was one of a number of little oases where travellers could find food, drink and a bed for the night.

Most taverns in the area at the time were little more than a tent with some crude bunks made of sticks, and these by all accounts were horribly uncomfortable. The place would also invariably have a fireplace of piled stones and a bar at one end. Here, hard men working on road construction, sheep drives and prospecting would gather to drink and fight themselves senseless on dodgy whiskey. Waking up the next morning with your vision still intact and most of your possessions was a bonus.

As our horde of cyclists passed through Jacksons a small crowd of onlookers had gathered to watch the race go by. They clapped and cheered and yelled encouragement. One voice stood out from the rest and proclaimed 'Keep it up, not long to go now.' I felt a quiver of excitement rise up within me. 'Wow, I am really doing it!'

Perhaps it was the realisation that we were nearly at the next transition point, or perhaps it was the fact that we had a small gallery of onlookers, but suddenly the pace picked up and in no time we were back to maximum speed again. I ducked as low as I could behind the rider in front of me to reduce my profile to the wind and hung on. The engine had woken up and was firing on all cylinders.

We sped down the small hills and raced across the flats. As the engine room got into their work the bunch started to thin out and it looked as if we would soon be in single file again and hanging on for dear life, when a familiar figure took the front. It was Mr Colossus.

His impact was immediate. With his considerable bulk at the front of the bunch, the other riders quickly realised that he afforded shelter of biblical proportions and soon the whole bunch had closed up. This was welcome relief. While still travelling at the same speed as before, we were now three or four abreast toward the rear. This provided us more protection and we took the rest appreciatively. Mr Colossus himself seemed reluctant to give up his spot at the business end of the bunch and fortunately for the rest of the strugglers like myself the engine room seemed happy to let him lead. I don't want to sound unkind here but it was not unlike cycling behind a bus. He kept up his effort for a number of minutes and when he did finally peel off and drift back the engine room was positively effusive in its nodded approval.

The break was soon over. In no time at all we were back into a long thin line as the engine room drove on. The long thin line, however, extended back only about twenty riders, at which point Mr Colossus sat sheltering the weak and the infirm (including myself) behind his greatness.

We could now sense that the end of the bike stage was very near. I looked at my speedo and saw it tick over at 52 kilometres. We only had three to go. The pace remained hot and I still had to work hard but I didn't mind too much. While I wanted to save my legs for the run I had come this far with the bunch and I wasn't going to drop off now.

For the first time in a while I looked around. The sun was shining and reflecting off the shiny spokes and wheel rims as we raced along to the glorious hum of the cycles. The mist that had clung so tightly to the surrounding hills was all but burnt away and up the road there wasn't a truck or a car to be seen. I began to feel quite euphoric. The ride had gone well. I had survived and in fact revelled in the speed of the much-dreaded Kumara downhill section; I had avoided crashes, intimidating passing manoeuvres and a virtual smorgasbord of food and cycle paraphernalia on the road. I'd met some new people, found strength I had no idea I possessed – and I had even momentarily led the bunch.

After so much pre-race worry and trepidation here I was riding along quite competently in a bunch situation. Sure, there had been a few tricky situations but as the last few kilometres ticked by I felt quite confident now that I was about to complete the first major stage of the Coast to Coast without further incident.

Within a few minutes we crossed the railway line that had been shadowing us since near Kumara, cycled around a bend and spread out in front of us was the transition point for the start of the run.

After the earthy colours of the countryside the scene before me seemed unreal. Under a banner announcing the end of the first stage, decked out in all the colours of the rainbow, were hundreds and hundreds of people of all shapes and sizes. There were support crews, officials, spectators and the remnants of a bunch that had arrived before us and mostly departed for the run. At the back of my bunch, as excited as a 10-year-old kid, I whizzed into the vibrant and colourful mêlée laid out in front of me. It was time for the circus to begin in earnest.

Chapter 10

Running on Empty

Just short of the finish banner I hit the brakes. I was so excited I could barely contain myself. Before my bike had stopped I threw my leg over the seat to dismount, intending to leap off it and bound through the transition area like a hungry leopard close to the kill. Instead I got off and began a most ungainly trot that must have resembled something more like a three-legged dressage pony. My legs felt all wrong. They seemed dull and I felt like I was trotting on stumps. There was no sensitivity to the ground. Each short step looked delicate enough but hit the ground hard and sent a jolt up my leg. What were my feet and toes up to? I couldn't feel them properly. I looked down but there were no obvious clues.

I looked up. Pushing my bike alongside me, I trotted into chaos. Ahead of me more than 50 riders were dragging their bikes through a chute that extended a hundred metres or so but was only five metres wide. The competitors charged through the narrow passage like the bulls in Palermo, handlebars ready to gore the unwary. On both sides were hundreds of highly agitated support crews straining on tiptoes looking for their competitors and yelling his or her name in hope that soon they would be united. At the same time competitors were yelling for their support crews, bleating like lost lambs.

Someone in front of me tripped and went down. A small pile-up ensued. Bikes were tangled and stuck. I reacted in time and skirted around.

In the middle of the chaos I briefly saw Robin Judkins grinning from ear to ear. He clearly loved every minute of this thing, this panicked mess he had created.

I felt assaulted by sound. There was confusion everywhere. Voices from every direction. 'Have you got your hat?' 'Dave, you dropped your banana!' 'Where are my shoes?' I hobbled past one competitor who was shouting in a booming voice for his support crew: 'Doug, Doug where the **** are you, you stupid prick?' Everywhere matches were being made. Time was precious. Find the crew, give them the bike, helmet off, gloves off. Grab the run bag. Go, go, go!

I trotted on right through the crowd of transitioning athletes and crew until almost at the end of the transition point and then I finally saw them. Chris, who must have already seen me, was waving and I nodded in confirmation that I had seen him.

Tony took the bike from me while I unclipped the helmet and gave it to Graham. The lads were ecstatic that I was still in one piece and said I was doing well. (Read: stunned that I had actually made it this far and hopeful that I might survive the rest of the day.)

I discarded the gloves and cycling glasses, grabbed a bottle and took a long drink. It was a pleasure to be able to complete a simple task like drinking without having to worry about the treacherous consequences of making a mistake while on a bicycle. I felt thirsty. I had not really had as much water as I should have on the bike ride and so I took another long drink. It felt great.

Around me runners were leaving all the time. I began to feel an urgency to go with them. I dropped the bottle, grabbed a banana and put it in the back pocket of my cycle top. I rushed to clip my running bag around my waist and put on my hat while Tony squirted sunblock all over my neck and ears.

I was ready to leave. I thanked my crew and turned to go. With a 'Take it easy to start with' and 'Good luck' they sent me on my way.

I ran through a farm gate and into an open field. There were small orange posts to mark the way and I jogged past them one by one. I was in no hurry. I knew I needed to work my way into the run and the best way was a slow beginning. I soon got to the other side of the field and as I did so the orange markers gave way to a farm track. Strung out ahead of me in ones and twos were members of the bunch I had cycled with. They plodded along in various states of wellbeing as their bodies adjusted to running and the demons of cycling progressively loosened their tenacious grip.

My legs still felt heavy and lifeless and it was as if I had iron bars strapped to each thigh. They had not recovered from the bike ride. With little feeling for the terrain I was thankful for the relatively even and flat vehicle track that curled its way up the valley.

With a feeling of general annoyance at my lack of co-ordination and a slight tinge of hunger I decided to seek solace in food and reached for my banana. It wasn't there. I realised I must have dropped it. I groaned in frustration.

A couple of other competitors passed me. I would have liked to have stayed with them but it was impossible. They were soon out of sight. It was depressing. However, as I rounded the next bend I saw not far ahead the only person who was probably running slower than I was. It was Mr Colossus.

Like me, he wasn't really running either. He was walking fast. I soon caught up to him but there is no benefit from drafting behind someone moving at just above walking pace so I drifted on by. I was grateful for his bulk on the bike and let him know.

'That was great work you did on the bike,' I offered.

'Oh, thanks,' he said, without looking up. 'But it's all irrelevant now.'

I left him for what was probably going to be a hell of a long and uncomfortable day... for both of us.

I looked at my watch. It was only 9am and I had already completed a three kilometre run, a 55-kilometre cycle ride and started on the 33-kilometre mountain run. It all seemed rather odd. It wasn't that long ago when the most exercise I had before 9am was to walk into my kitchen and make a cup of tea. I realised some aspects of my life had undergone a remarkable change. For example, over the previous year I had become aware that time was precious. Thirty minutes could either be spent sitting on my butt in front of the television or jogging around my neighbourhood. Instead of 15 minutes reading of the woes of the world in the newspaper (is there anything more truly depressing?), I could spend time throwing a ball with my son.

After running for 10 minutes or so I began to ease into a bit of a rhythm and running became more pleasant. The track straightened ahead and I could see the western end of the footbridge over the Otira River. I knew I must soon turn hard left and cross the river. No competitors were allowed to use the bridge. It had a maximum safety limit of one person at a time and there would have been huge delays. Besides, it was not in the spirit of the event. Rivers were to be waded. One must feel the icy clench of the freezing river on one's genitals or the outdoor experience was somehow lessened. No one in this race was allowed to miss this dubious thrill.

As I approached the bridge a small group of lithe-looking runners came past. I immediately recognised the first of them. His name was Chris Cox. Chris was something of a Coast to Coast legend. He competed in the first race in 1983 and he had been over the run more times than anyone else in the history of the race. Chris took groups of paying customers over the run course almost every weekend in summer.

Rumour has it, however, that Chris doesn't share all his secrets with the paying public. Some say he keeps a few to himself and maybe select clients. From time to time he can be seen personally guiding one or other of the race contenders over the mountain alone. Of course the next best thing to personal tuition was to follow him on race day. If you could keep up, that is. Obviously the six men on his heels were trying to do just that.

I watched them pass the footbridge and then benefited from some fortuitous timing. Instead of following the runners ahead Chris suddenly turned left and disappeared into the bush above the river. His disciples followed. I arrived at the spot where they had turned. The shrubs and bushes were quite densely packed but there was a discernable path. As I hesitated others ran past me continuing up the track toward the better-known crossing point a considerable distance further on. Feeling uncertain, I decided to risk it and followed the short, narrow path down to the river bed.

I looked up to see the last of the disciples was chest-deep in the river. I had a quick decision to make. Go with them immediately or dither about and cross alone. Without thinking more than that if I was going into water chest deep I didn't want to do it alone, I charged into the water.

The cold took my breath away. My legs went numb, my fingers froze and other parts of my anatomy curled up and hid. It was cold and I just wanted out.

Chris and his disciples were obviously late for something and were disappearing across the riverbed at an alarming rate and as much as I wanted to stay with them and rejoice in future shortcuts I knew I could never keep up. I found a rough dirt track and followed it. It wove its way between prickly gorse bushes (thank you very bloody much, English colonists) and up the left-hand bank of the Deception River. After the gorse bushes thinned out the track continued through a rocky field of short grass.

Ahead of me were plenty of other runners and I hoped at least a few of them would still be about further on when I reached the more complicated sections where I had heard the track was difficult to follow.

A few minutes later and I was back in the dry riverbed. The track was now almost as smooth as a gravel road and although I stretched out a little to raise my speed the further I ran the more I began to feel my performance was declining. I didn't feel quite right.

I continued on for ten minutes or so, lost in my own little world of discomfort, but soon after began to notice an increase in the numbers of runners passing me. I found that as more and more runners came by my disappointment turned to anger. And this despite the fact that most were extremely friendly and nearly all passed by with a friendly 'Hi there' or a genuine 'How's it going'.

My thoughts began to slide into an abyss of negativity. Who were all these people? Why were they all going so much damn faster than me and why were they being so bloody nice about it? Here I was struggling away just as hard as everyone else but I still couldn't keep up. I stewed away to myself, perfectly aware that my feelings were totally unreasonable and at the same time feeling unable to stop them. It was the comments that riled me the most. It was as if there was a sign on me that said 'Incompetent runner, please pass with consoling comment'. Every time someone said 'How are you doing' I felt like saying 'Well I was fine until you passed me, why don't you piss off back to where you came from and mind your own business?'

I tried to shift my focus to something more constructive. As I picked my way through a tricky section of rocks I tried to concentrate on my foot placement as a way of focusing my mind but it didn't seem to help. As I plodded on I soon found my thoughts wandering back to the dark side.

I became aware of someone else running close behind me. I looked around and saw it was a thin, wiry chap who was probably in his mid 50s. He grinned but said nothing. I nodded politely. It was a small triumph considering how I felt. We ran on in silence.

A short while later we reached a point where we had to cross the Deception River to avoid a bluff. As we got part-way across we simultaneously realised the water was moving swiftly so we linked arms. Being the bigger of the two of us I took the upstream side as we lumbered into the main flow.

The rocks below the surface were only partially visible owing to the churning of the surface water. This complicated the crossing but we staggered about feeling our way with our feet.

Now I have never been much for crossing rivers but compared to the thin, wiry chap I was an expert. He somehow managed to lose his footing twice but both times I was able to steady him. We crossed without further incident.

'Thanks,' he said. 'I'm not much good in rivers.'

'You don't say,' I replied under my breath.

I was not in the mood for conversation.

We ran on a few hundred metres and crossed back over the river to take advantage of a long, grassy river flat. The river was wider and the crossing much easier. Well for me it was. The wiry chap staggered about like a blind man and even tripped and fell over in about two inches of water. He would have been the sort of child that scared the hell out of his parents at the beach. The kind of kid that is not allowed near the water unless he's wearing a self-righting lifejacket with a strobe light and a siren that goes off when it tips over.

Once out of the main flow I drank a few mouthfuls of the cool fresh water by cupping my hands together. It gave me a momentary lift but it soon passed. I trudged on. I was starting to feel very weak and wasn't sure I could continue running once across the river. I wondered depressingly if I would have to walk the rest of the journey.

I sighed heavily as we walked up the far bank. My new companion following close behind could sense I was struggling.

'When did you last eat?' he asked.

The question took me by surprise. We had barely crossed a river together and he was already asking personal questions about my dietary habits. I decided to answer anyway.

'Um, on the bike I think.' I couldn't actually remember.

There was a short silence.

'It's important to eat often in this race,' was all he said.

I thought about it. I had got a little caught up in things and I was quite hungry.

'Yeah, probably a good idea,' I replied. I swivelled my running bag around in front of me and started searching through it as it bounced up and down in rhythm with my steps. I had plenty of things to choose from but decided to start with a gluggy little sachet of sugary sports gel. Once I'd gulped the sticky beast down and pried my jaws apart again I was ready for some real food.

I managed to eat an energy bar and some nuts before I tired from trying to eat, run and breathe at the same time. Breathing became the priority.

The food however had done its job. Within five minutes I was feeling much better and my pace started to pick up.

Chapter 11

Bouncing Back

I introduced myself properly to the wiry chap, who turned out to be an accountant named Steve. He took over the lead for a while and we got talking as we ran. Steve was doing his second Coast to Coast but he had also done a few marathons, swimming triathlons and some mountain bike racing. He had a lot of experience and we talked about all sorts of things.

I told him how I had been feeling lousy and he explained that more often than not this was because athletes didn't eat and drink enough or at the right times.

Anyone who called me an athlete was either a very nice person or just plain stupid. I began to like him.

Steve went on to explain that it was vital to eat and drink at least small amounts regularly even if you didn't always feel like it. He also explained how important it was to eat and drink in the first half-hour after finishing. This significantly improved your chances of recovering well and being able to enjoy the second day of the race.

I learnt other things as well: Don't buy new shoes just before the race; it's better to be slightly undertrained than overtrained by race day; eat the same foods during training that you intend to eat during the race; silicon tires for your road bike are worth the extra cost and clip-in cycle shoes are definitely the way to go; Vaseline on your nipples can save you from getting a nasty rash; drink sachets from the supermarket are a cheap and useful source of fuel; the equivalent of a glass of water every 20 minutes during the race will ensure you keep properly hydrated. If Steve were a handbook on racing in the outdoors I would have bought him there and then. And as long as he never mentioned anything about the correct way to cross a river I would have accepted just about anything he said.

I ate a little more. I began to feel really good.

Now that I was running behind him I couldn't help but notice it felt easier than when I was leading myself. I simply looked at his heels and stepped where he stepped. This proved a very efficient way to travel. I had no need to look up and make decisions about where to go because he was doing that. This freed me up to concentrate on where my foot needed to be next. I mentioned this to Steve and he said it was an important observation. Following another runner was a useful saving in time and energy and a common practice among the elite. Steve told me that if you didn't have someone directly in front of you to follow you could still track them quite easily by looking for wet footprints and gravel on rocks ahead. This, he said, helped make it easier to decide on where to place your foot or when to cross the river (which we seemed to be forever in and out of).

Steve also made me feel better about my competitive instincts. He said that for him the Coast to Coast was not so much a race as a personal journey. He said initially he found it wasn't hard to lose sight of that when he was passing or being passed by people but he decided at the end of the day where he came was irrelevant as long as he enjoyed the challenge and made it to the finish.

I ran with Steve for close to half an hour but it seemed much less. We crossed the river three or four more times and in exchange for keeping him alive at each crossing he continued to dispense good advice. We made good progress up the valley. After one particularly adventurous crossing we came out of the water into the cool shadow of native bush where there was a strong smell of sulphur in the air. It was difficult to tell exactly where it was coming from but it was clear there was some kind of geothermal activity somewhere nearby. It was exciting to be in such an interesting and raw environment.

Steve was enjoying himself too. Even though he had only been over the course a few times he found that he was still remembering much of it as he ran. Sometimes, however, his memory wouldn't kick in until the last possible second before a decision had to be made. It was navigation by distant memory and it was fun.

We hugged the bush-clad banks as we ran around and between quite large rocks. We rounded a bend, ducked under a tree branch and came to halt on a small gravel beach. On our left was an unclimbable bluff and on our right the river. Directly in front of us was a pool of water, and at the end, a large rock. I was at a bit of a loss as to where to go but Steve wasn't. He looked at the wet gravel at his feet and with an, 'Oh, that's right,' he charged straight into the pool of water. Wading chest-deep in the water to the rock, he then scrambled up and over it using foot and handholds that were difficult to see from where I stood. I followed quickly not wanting to be left behind, found the necessary holds and forged on. The rock was no problem but when I came down the other side Steve met me with a warning.

'Be really careful here.' I looked ahead and saw what looked like no more than a few metres of rocks that were wetted by a small side-creek. My first two steps revealed the reason for the warning. The rocks were like soap. Despite the warning I still managed to fall once before making the safety of the other side.

We were now at the beginning of a large grassy plain. The river veered over to the right and as we ran on following a well-trodden path we left the river altogether. It was pleasant running.

The path eventually petered out altogether at an empty river braid but we continued to run in the general direction the track was heading last time we saw it. Soon the river crossed our path again as it made its way to the left-hand side of the plain. We made quick progress and crossed where it was wide and shallow but somehow Steve still managed to trip and fall. This guy was a legend.

Once across, there was still no discernable path to follow but fortunately the ground was flat and the stones were small so the running was good everywhere. As I looked around I started to notice small groups of runners and the odd individual all over the place but generally heading upstream. Clearly opinions on the best route varied. We did notice, however, that we had made big gains on the groups and individuals who chose to run further out to the left where it looked like the rocks and stones were bigger.

Towards the end of the plain the mountains closed in, almost touching the sides of the river. The number of route choices gradually fell to two. It was either the left bank of the river or the right. We chose the right.

For the next while the route opened out into more flats but they were never as wide or as long. For a while we ran in the riverbed alongside the water. I noticed from the marks and debris on the banks that where we were running had been well under water at some time in the past. Judging by the size of some of the dead trees that had come to rest beside the river the volume and fury of the water must have been a sight to behold. Certainly no passage up-river would have been possible. In fact I imagined that even a small increase in water volume would have hindered our progress considerably as we would have had to run a much more difficult line hard up against the riverbank.

We soon came across a small cairn. This little man-made pile of rocks marked a well-hidden entrance to a bush track. The track itself was as smooth as a footpath and made for pleasant running. We were able to make much faster progress than if we had been clambering over the football-sized rocks in the riverbed.

In fact as we came out the other end of the track and were back beside the water I looked downstream and could see a group of three slowly navigating their way up to where we were. I realised this was the second occasion that morning I had saved considerable time and maybe even improved a few places through a lucky route choice. While I was very pleased and got a little psychological lift each time it happened I couldn't help but wonder how many other shortcuts I had missed.

As we started a gradual climb Steve began to pull ahead. He noticed and stopped, waiting for me to catch up. When I did catch up I said it didn't seem right for him to wait and that he should go on ahead and enjoy his adventure at his own pace. He understood and we shook hands.

For all the advice he gave me I only had one piece for him. I encouraged him not to cross anything more than a trickle of water by himself. He took it well.

With a cheery 'Good luck' he was off and was soon way ahead. The speed with which he put distance between us surprised me. I realised that he had been more than charitable staying with me as long as he did.

And as I moved up into the rocky upper reaches of the Deception I felt more confident. I ran the next section deliberately, slowly and in a measured way because as I looked ahead I could see the track was beginning to climb. While my pace was slow and my heart rate high I was not discouraged. I was now more determined than ever. It was as if the seriousness of my intent had begun to match the increasingly stark environment.

The valley narrowed considerably and the vegetation was now more or less restricted to the steep slopes of the mountains on either side while the valley floor consisted of fields of river stone. From time to time I would fight my way through a small grove of shrubs to emerge into another long yet narrow field of stones stretching into the distance.

There was quite a clear path through this area. It seemed strange that one of the most clearly defined sections of track I had seen thus far was over such a seemingly impressionless surface of rock and stone. Yet there it was, with its faint outline directly in front of me but becoming clearer the further it stretched off into the distance. It seemed that the rocks and stones in the upper Deception River valley were slightly discoloured by some kind of lichen or moss and over the years the boots and shoes of runners and trampers had gradually worn a faint but discernable path.

This made me think about something I had not contemplated before: that even the smallest impression of man on nature, even a footprint on rock, can still be felt. And while I consider myself a conservationist I wasn't too upset. There is always going to be some price for access.

As I continued to run I noticed that the track stretching before me was forced to head back toward the river by the encroaching mountain slopes. Looking up the valley it appeared as if there would be little room for any river flats ahead.

The river had gouged out its own path on its way down the valley. In some places it had gouged out more than in others, exposing large boulders and leaving the water well below the steep rocky banks. As I ran alongside I took care not to misplace a step as the drop to the water had grown in the last few minutes from almost nothing to about two metres. I didn't feel entirely comfortable running here and it soon got worse.

I came out of a small stand of bush and scrub to see a massive rock fan blocking the way. This huge pile of rocks, stones and gravel had probably tumbled down the mountainside over many years but curiously had stopped just short of the river. It did not appear to encroach into the river at all. That is not to say that at some point in time it wasn't going to. A small earthquake would probably send the whole gigantic pile smashing into the water. As far as I was concerned this might happen at any time.

Imagine, then, my horror when I noticed my beloved track winding its way along the face of the giant rock slide like the path of a surfer across a huge wave.

The speed of my running dropped along with my confidence as I approached the rock slide. I almost ground to a complete halt on the edge as I surveyed the path ahead. Ordinarily when confronted with an obstacle like this my thoughts have revolved around the theory that turning back and going home is the best option, but not today. I had to get across if I was to continue the race.

I made up my mind. I needed to get across quickly to minimise my exposure to the danger, therefore I decided to run like a crazy bastard and hope that in his infinite wisdom God would not decide to give the Arthur's Pass region a bloody good shaking in the next few minutes.

So off I went scrambling across the rock slide in a semi-controlled panic. Running like a crazy bastard is usually a fine theory on flat ground but here it was complicated by the fact that a single misplaced foot could see me falling to an inglorious end in the river. I strained to see all the obstacles in front of me – the sweat was running down into my eyes – and eventually succeeded in whacking my shin on a protruding rock I hadn't seen. I barely noticed the pain as I scurried on. I was in headlong pursuit of safe ground and nothing short of losing a leg was going to stop me.

A few seconds later my top got caught on a stick and raised my panic level a couple of notches until it wrenched free with a crack as the stick broke. Released, I shot forward like an arrow from a bow.

I noticed that each time the track went up near the top of the slide my head would be just above the line of the rock slide. I felt more vulnerable than ever. I was convinced that if indeed God chose this day to end my life I could be neatly decapitated by a single rock and there would be no need for him to go to the effort of bringing down the entire rock slide.

I scrambled over the last few metres of ground in a very undignified manner, grunting like a pig and snorting loudly but finally I arrived at the other side. The sense of relief was almost overwhelming. It's incredibly hard work rushing headlong across a dangerous rock slide whilst simultaneously catering for all one's fears and I took a few moments to collect myself.

The quiet gurgle of the river and the sound of my gasping were soon interrupted by the sound of voices from behind me. I turned to see a woman in the company of two men just starting to cross the rock slide. Despite the hostile surroundings I could hear them chatting away happily. They seemed to be taking the crossing in a remarkably relaxed manner. They couldn't have seen the danger.

As they got closer I felt the urge to get moving again. I wasn't quite ready to throw away my competitiveness just yet, not while there was life still in me. I turned and carried on up the track at a brisk walk. It was all I could manage for the present.

I soon came to a section of huge boulders. The river wound its way between them and swirled angrily where its passage was thwarted. The track was less obvious now and I found the best way to navigate was to look for the cairn that appeared every 50 metres or so. There seemed to be multiple options to get from one cairn to the next so each time I arrived at a cairn I chose what looked like the easiest route toward the next one and headed off.

A few minutes later the terrain steepened sharply and I climbed up and away from the river. I became aware of rushing water ahead of me and realised that, coming from that direction, it couldn't be from the Deception River. I climbed over a series of rocky outcrops and suddenly arrived at a significant side creek. It was Doreen Creek. In front of me water was flooding down from my right and meeting with the main flow of the Deception River on my left and 10 metres below. On the other side of Doreen Creek was a loose collection of people that for a moment I thought were athletes I had somehow magically caught up to but on closer inspection turned out to be some of the official race photographers and media.

By very cautiously jumping from boulder to boulder I picked my way across the creek to where they were. I felt quite self-conscious and took special care not to provide the media with any embarrassing pictures that might end up in the national papers under the headline, 'Man Hurt In Famous Race – Buttocks In Plaster.'

Once across the creek I had no idea where to go. The Deception River was now well down to my left and passage up it looked near-impossible. Up and to my right Doreen Creek thundered down angrily among huge rocks. Just in case I had taken leave of my senses and wanted to head off in that direction the whole river was taped off from bank to bank with the word 'Danger' appearing every few inches. Directly in front of me, looking less ominous but still quite impassable, was a small rock face. Above the rock face was a wall of native bush. Not wanting to seem as incompetent as I was feeling, I started to dawdle in the direction of the rock face hoping that either it would magically open up before me or provide some other clue as to where I should go.

As there were no other runners to observe, the whole contingent of photographers and media watched me closely as I ever-so-slowly approached the wall. I felt their eyes boring into me. What the hell was I going to do, run into the wall? Suddenly one of the photographers leapt up what were obviously well-used steps and hand-holds in the rock face in front of me, before turning to take my photo from the small plateau at the top. He had unwittingly shown me the way. I charged up the face after him as if I had done it a thousand times before and grinned as he took my picture.

Chapter 12

Doreen Creek to Goat Pass

For the first time I was in the bush proper. It was darker out of the direct sunlight, and I welcomed the coolness. The track, although winding around trees, over stumps, through small bogs and sometimes seemingly through bushes rather than around them, was nevertheless clearly visible underfoot. It started climbing almost as soon as I entered the bush and soon I had left Doreen Creek far behind. From time to time I could hear the Deception as it raged away to my left and far below where I could not see it. For the first time in the race I was quite alone. I liked it. The only noises I could hear were my breathing and the slop of my shoes in the shallow stream of water that was using the track as its own route to the river.

The track levelled off for a while and then started to climb in a zig-zag fashion further up the hillside before starting to work its way around the side again. I crossed a couple of small creeks in which the rocks were hellishly slippery, but without incident.

I tried gamely for the sake of comfort to skirt around the side of a boggy patch of mud that dominated the track in front of me but failed dismally, losing my footing and sliding into its squelching depths. I withdrew my foot hoping that my shoe would still be attached to it. It was, but came out of the mud with a sound that would not be acceptable in polite company.

I carried on but soon noticed that after being in the mud my left shoe weighed at least twice as much as my right. This did not help my running. I stumbled up the track dragging my heavy left leg. The mud stank and it felt like my leg was shackled to a smelly iron ball. Gradually, however, the mud fell away until the only evidence of its presence was the brown tide-mark up to my shin and a lingering stench.

I learnt the lesson and for the next few minutes navigated my way around the more ugly-looking bogs with great care.

Next I had to contend with slippery tree roots and damp, moss-laden rocks. After that it was soft, dark soil that clung to my shoes and made each step on a tree root treacherous. It was difficult but I was enjoying myself. This was what I had come for. Adventure.

The nature of the bush began to change. As the canopy of the trees above thickened the bush took on a gloomier feel. Long vines hung down from the tree limbs as if groping for passers-by to pull toward the light. Ferns and punga trees reached up from the floor to meet them. Wherever they met they entwined as if locked in a soulful embrace.

Gloomy green was all around me. The only reprieves from the dull sea of green were where tiny shafts of sunlight broke through the canopy, illuminating dust and insect life that momentarily passed through the long narrow beams.

As I jogged on I heard voices and laughter somewhere up ahead of me. It sounded like a sizeable group were just out of sight. I ran hard for the next few minutes to catch up with them. After a few minutes I was breathing heavily. I gave up the chase and began walking, puzzled that I hadn't managed to catch them. I walked on, lost in thought, and came over the brow of a small rise, from where I heard the chatter and laughing of the group again, only this time much closer. Almost smiling at the thought of having company again I charged on through a large patch of ferns down into the next small valley and fought my way through some bushes and out the other side, only to find I was still alone. There was no sign of the group. I stopped and listened but heard nothing. There was virtually no sound at all bar the distant murmur of the Deception way down to my left. Even the birds were quiet. It was quite uncanny.

'Gidday,' said a voice behind me.

I jumped in fright.

'Crikey, where did you come from?' I stammered as I tried to compose myself.

It was the two men and the woman I had seen crossing the rock face before Doreen Creek.

'Sorry, did we give you a fright? We've been trying to catch up with you for a while,' said the woman.

'Oh,' was all I could manage. There was an awkward silence.

As if led by some unknown force we all realised at the same time that we had paused for long enough and without another word we moved off. The two men took the lead and soon we were moving quite quickly. The track continued to be hard work as we fought our way over rocks and boulders and through the shrubs that grew between them. With less route finding to do I began to enjoy myself again. The three of them progressed up the valley in a way that suited me. They ran on the flat and downhill sections, walked up the steep and hilly parts and recovered when necessary before breaking into a trot again. In a short time we covered a lot more ground than I would have alone and soon we were catching up with a group in front. From time to time I would catch glimpses of them about 50 metres ahead before they disappeared round a bend or through a stand of small trees. I assumed they were the mystery group that I had been chasing earlier without success. We were clearly catching them but it never happened.

A few minutes later we saw the last of them go around a bend in the track, but when we got to the point where we had last seen them they were no longer there. They had followed a rather steep track down the slope toward the Deception River.

We did not follow them. Instead, one of the two men in our group turned to the remaining three of us, put his finger to his lips and went 'Shh!' With a sneaky glint in his eye he then turned his back on us and took a couple of steps before disappearing through a veil of shrubs and bushes. Another secret path!

I looked down to see the last of the mystery group well below us disappearing through the trees just above the river. I left them to it and charged through the veil of greenery after my new companions. After a few annoying scratches and a one-sided fight with an aggressive tree branch that poked me in the neck (I took retribution and broke the swine) I emerged to find myself on what was obviously a well-hidden shortcut. I pushed on as quickly as I could safely manage. While the surface of the track was good in places the surrounding bushes forced their leaves onto the track space in their quest for sunlight. It was almost impossible to see exactly where you were placing your foot. It was not unlike wading through dirty water: it was probably going to be fine but there was just a possibility your next step might be into a nasty hole.

Excited by the potential gains of the shortcut, we made great haste. The track continued to wind its way further around the hillside and we found ourselves running in close formation as fast as we dared all the while ducking and weaving to avoid branches, rocks, stumps and other obstacles.

In only a few minutes we were out on the banks of the upper Deception River. It was nice to be out in the sunshine again and the early morning chill was well and truly gone. I looked down to where I suspected the mystery group would eventually appear but saw no one. My best guess was that ours was a more direct route and had led to a considerable saving in time and effort. My guess was confirmed not long after when I looked back again and saw the lead runners of the mystery group a distant couple of hundred metres back and climbing slowly up to where we had come out of the bush.

As we continued to make our way up the valley the terrain began to change again. The walls of the slopes closed in even more and there was no option but to run close to the river. From time to time we were forced to follow the track through some sections where the surrounding vegetation was almost impregnable.

The bushes surrounding us were a little above head-height and we found that if we ran upright we were constantly fighting to get through them. The alternative was to stoop over and run in the narrow channel that existed from the ground to about shoulder height directly above the track. If you ran upright it was like, I imagined, running with your face between two cheese graters. If you stooped over to avoid this painful experience it was a hell of a strain on your back, and I worried that if I should trip while in this most vulnerable position, since I was effectively already halfway to the ground I would most likely lunge forward to a most unpleasant face-altering and teeth-smashing doom. The pressure of running with a group prompted me to resolve on a sort of stooped walk punctuated with wild bursts of speed to ensure I didn't lose touch with the others. For the sake of my back I had to stand up every now and then and fight my way through the greenery, all the while thinking how much I would give for an industrial-strength weed whacker.

I kept my eyes on the ground and used my peaked cap to protect my head from the slap of leaves and branches. I was basically running blind and at some stage the peak of the cap must have obscured a sharp tree branch because something gouged into my forehead as I ran into it. I felt a bit dazed but carried on. The next time we slowed to a walk the others oohed and aahed and said there was blood running down my face. I had been concentrating so hard and been so caught up in the running I hadn't noticed it. I pulled off my cap to locate the source that apparently (I thankfully couldn't see it) was a nasty cut. My companions patched it up with a sticking plaster from my bag and we carried on. I was starting feel that I was having way more than my fair share of bad luck when the woman running behind me slipped and whacked her shin on a rock. I wouldn't go as far as to say I was delighted but the first thing that crossed my mind was that it was nice that it wasn't me for a change. I decided not to share this thought with her as she howled in pain and we attempted to console her.

She recovered soon enough and we ran further up the valley. We ran on the right-hand side of the river for some time before coming to a point where we needed to cross. The day had got quite hot and I was amazed at how good it felt to have my tiring legs in the cool refreshing water. I cupped my hands together and drank a few mouthfuls and threw some over my head and neck. It was, and I'm quite aware that I might sound as if I am getting carried away here, a simply divine experience.

Once we had crossed over we followed the wet footprints and fine gravel on the rocks. From time to time there were short, well-used tracks that led us briefly out of the river around a large rock or along the bank for a few metres or so but then returned to the river. The sneaky bloke who was leading us would groan each time we took one of these short diversions and came back out onto the river. He explained that these short tracks were 'high-water tracks' and while they were a quicker option when the level of the water in the river was high, when it was low they were simply a waste of precious time. It was faster, he said, to travel on the dry verge of the riverbed than in the water and so this was predominantly where we ran.

We clambered from rock to rock at what seemed to me a remarkable speed considering the risks. A bad slip, trip or misjudgement could have easily resulted in a twisted ankle or worse.

I followed the others closely and managed to keep up. My only physical discomfort was cramp in my left hamstring. It had been occurring each time I overstretched when trying to leap between rocks. Its return made me feel tentative and reluctant to fully stretch out. I avoided big leaps for a while and the cramp left me alone, but I began to realise what I could have done better in training to prepare myself.

For a start I should have run the course. There could be no better preparation because at the end of the day training is simply showing your body and your mind what it needs to do on the day of the race. True, I had dabbled in the pursuits associated with the Coast to Coast, but I could now see I was well short of adequate preparation. Even if I hadn't run the course there was plenty I could have done at home to prepare without even leaving the property.

For example, I could have ridden for two hours in the garage on my bike machine while periodically being snuck up on and whacked with a piece of bamboo. Let me explain.

The cycling on the machine would of course approximately replicate the effort required to cycle 55 kilometres. The added complication of having to keep a lookout for the surprise attacker with a bamboo cane would be an excellent replication of the need for vigilance on the bike. How else could one prepare for the horrific state of fear and anxiety felt whilst cycling in a bunch knowing that if you weren't awake to every nuance of the bunch your flesh could go from being pink and rosy one minute to shredded to all hell and full of gravel the next?

Once off the machine I could have quickly changed into running gear and lurched off into the backyard. It would be necessary to fill the children's swimming pool with ice-cold water so I could sit down in it a minute to replicate the shock of the river crossings. To add a touch of realism I could have tensed my leg muscles as tightly as possible to try and cause cramp. After this I could have trudged around the backyard for hour after hour while every now and then helpers tried to scratch my face and legs with tree branches. I could have climbed over pieces of garden furniture, leapt over children's toys, jumped off the wheelbarrow and then run into the house and up the stairs in an attempt to replicate the frequent climbs. I could have filled my shoes with mud and I could have run stooped over. At least some of this preparation would have been useful.

Instead I took a different path. Most of the time I cycled alone and at a leisurely pace. I enjoyed the views and took in the surroundings. If I passed a pleasant café I stopped for coffee. I ran around the streets and in a gently undulating pine forest wearing dry shoes and socks. I ran in flat open parks with manicured grass and flowers growing on the verge. I ran amongst trees where the lowest branches were five metres off the ground. I followed tracks that were so wide you could run 10 abreast with impunity. I crossed rivers via bridges and I kept away from hills as much as possible. The longest I had run for was two hours and 20 minutes.

If the race was a short unhurried bike ride followed by a sedate one-hour run at a leisurely pace, on manicured grass in a park of wild flowers and well trimmed trees and punctuated with periodic coffee breaks, I would have been fine. Unfortunately it was not like that at all. I had been running now for a little over two hours and I wasn't yet at the halfway point.

When the river became almost impassable with huge rocks and deep pools fed by waterfall after waterfall we left the verge and followed an obvious track up the left-hand bank. It led us through a section of the sharpest rocks I had ever seen. These rocks were quite distinctive from any others I had encountered on the run so far. Not only for their orange tinge, but also they looked as though they had been chiselled by hand and carefully placed with a sharp end sticking up, much like a collection of church spires. But there was nothing holy about them.

While ahead of me there was no pathway in the traditional sense, the way across was clear. Each pinnacle, each stepping stone on the path, was well worn in the same way as the stony path I had travelled earlier down in the valley.

The four of us picked our way gingerly through. There was no question of running. It was a time for caution. With great care we were soon across the razor rocks without major mishap.

The track beyond led us almost immediately back down to the verge of the water. As we ran on over the rocks we continued to climb up the valley. Most of the time it wasn't obvious to me that we were climbing until I looked back. Then I would look down to a point where I had been only a few minutes before and find myself surprised at how far below it now was.

There were other more subtle indications that we were climbing. One was the gradual end to conversation and another was the slow burning sensation that developed in my thighs. The longer we went on the worse it got until I found it difficult to keep running at all. I slowed to a walk and tried to recover. The less effort I put in the more I recovered but there was a cost: I began to notice that I was losing touch with the other three. At first I lagged behind just a few metres, then it was a few more until I knew I wasn't really up to their level of fitness. I thought I might come right if I just hung in there and kept trying but I was kidding myself. They were slowly pulling away from me. For the second time that morning I was forced to watch members of a bunch I was very keen to stay with disappearing up the track and taking valuable route secrets with them.

Just how valuable was brought home to me shortly afterward when I came to a point where on either side of the river were very steep banks. From what I could make out it looked like I had only one choice. I had to run up the river, in the water.

I hesitated. I couldn't get my head around the idea that the track was actually in the river. I looked all around searching for clues but found none. In desperation I looked back up the river and there it was: a splash of water over a partially submerged rock. Clearly someone had been past this point in the last few minutes. I looked further ahead and noticed a small but unmistakable cairn of stones on a sizeable rock. I knew this had to be the way and so before my watery markers dried in the sun I forged ahead into the river in search of more.

There was no clear path to follow but I made my own way taking the easiest route possible toward the cairn. On the way I noticed a footprint or two and the odd splash of water on otherwise dry rocks that told me others had passed this way.

Although I had found the water quite refreshing on earlier crossings I had never spent more than a few seconds in it as I whipped across. This was different. I worried that I was probably going to be wading in the cold water for some time and wondered if my feet might go numb.

I was pleasantly surprised, however, when I discovered after a few minutes wading that I had pretty much adjusted to the temperature and it didn't seem as cold as before. There was of course one exception: as

Enjoying the shade among sofa-size boulders, halfway up the creek to Goats Pass. Paul's Camera Shop

Sporting all the colours of the rainbow a huge bunch barrels down the road, closely observed by media in vans alongside. Michael Jacques

Taking a shortcut on the mountain run. Michael Jacques

One wrong step can mean trouble. It's all eyes down at one of the many river crossings on the Coast to Coast. Michael Jacques

A group of runners crossing Goat Pass at 1,070 metres. It's all downhill from here! Michael Jacques

Support crews and spectators await the first runners at Klondyke Corner. Although it's midsummer, in the distance there are still patches of snow on the peaks surrounding Goat Pass. Mark Elliott

Crossing Goat Pass. Despite the presence of the boardwalks a quick look around reminds you that this is wilderness. Michael Jacques

Still grinning... just. Near the top of Dudleys Knob, with Mount Oates (2,008 metres) over my left shoulder. Paul's Camera Shop

Calm before the storm. Support crews mill about the rows of kayaks waiting for their athletes to arrive as the first rays of sunlight flicker over the distant peaks.
Mark Nicol

It's all on. At the water's edge, support crews rush to launch their competitors, while beyond them those already afloat take their first tentative strokes in what for many will be a journey into the unknown. Mark Nicol

One of these kayakers is not like the others. Mike Ward, former Green Party MP, the only person to do every Coast to Coast, strains to see what's next while around him others are in their own private battles for survival. Paul's Camera Shop

There's a fine line between an exhilarating ride down a rapid and disaster! Paul's Camera Shop

Shattered! Struggling down the finishing chute at Sumner beach. The face says it all. Paul's Camera Shop

long as the 'refreshing' water stayed well clear of my groin region I could cope with almost anything.

I wound my way around sofa-sized rocks, clinging to the side of them as I did and stepping cautiously, not always sure where I was placing my foot because the water was so agitated. I continued to pick my way upstream, wading in one of the braids up the right-hand edge of the main flow.

I made good progress. The river flow was broken into so many small braids that forward progression against the flow was not a problem. But it didn't last. The further I travelled up the river the more difficult it became to cross as the water channelled with great force between the rocks.

Coming around a small bend I was confronted by one particularly large rock. To my left was the river and to the right an unclimbable bank. From what I could make out my only options were to try and scratch my way around it like a crab or to climb over it. The water looked alarmingly swift as it powered past the left-hand edge of the rock. I briefly considered jumping in but it was so swift I was sure I would be in for a thrashing if I got knocked off balance. I decided to take the conservative option. After a short but strenuous climb over the top and a difficult climb down the other side I finally passed the obstacle. It seemed a massive effort for gaining a total distance of a few metres and an overall height gain of about an inch!

As I caught my breath I was gutted to see two older men suddenly come around the river side of the rock I had just climbed over. Their grins told me that they had seen me climb over the rock. I determined to be more aggressive in future.

I was in and out of the river relentlessly as I crept up toward Goat Pass. I could tell by the way the ridge to my left was beginning to drop down in the direction I was heading that the pass could not be too far away.

The rugged beauty of my surroundings amazed me. Up above me towered huge craggy bluffs. I stared up at them in awe. Amongst the harsh, bare rock were large pockets of native flax and grasses that clung to the impossibly steep face. It was so high I almost fell over as I leant back to look up. I had never been in a place like this before. Standing there, knee deep in cold water in the shade of this stupendous bluff it was hard not to feel insignificant. I wavered there for a moment longer, taking in the sheer horror of it all before paranoia intervened to drive me away with thoughts of falling rocks. I scurried on and was soon out of the shade of the bluffs altogether.

I was now much closer to the pass and a quite different-looking U-shaped alpine valley began to open up before me. Even the river seemed considerably more amiable as it meandered down the much gentler slope toward me. The endless shrubs and bushes gave way to low tussock and alpine grasses and I was now able to run much more quickly and make better time.

Running now on the right of the river, I laboured up two short, stony rises before I gasped my way around a sharp bend. I followed the track as it dropped abruptly down in two long steps to the river and stopped dead. Yet again I had no idea where to go next.

I looked up the river. There was no identifiable track and I couldn't see any cairns. Although previously I had run long sections without confirmation that I was on the right course, I was still a little worried. I looked across the river for the continuation of the track. I couldn't see where it might possibly go. There was a very steep, rough bank of mud, rocks and tussock that extended about 10 metres up to some scrub and large flax bushes on what I assumed was the edge of a small plateau. Ordinarily I would not have considered this a possible route, but at the top of the bank I suddenly saw the perfect track marker. It was an iron pole.

It had to be the way. It was about as out of place as a deckchair in the Arctic. Crossing the river marked not only a major change in direction but also in terrain. Any further progress would be up a steep incline. From the river's edge it was possible to just make out a faint zig-zag route that wound its way up toward the pole. The zig-zag was steep and I walked up it slowly. Near the top I stopped briefly to catch my breath and looked about. I could see other runners slowly making their way across the river where I had crossed a few hundred metres back. I was tempted to wait for the company but they still had quite a way to go to reach me so I decided not to. They would probably catch me soon enough anyway.

Beyond the point where the runners were crossing the river were the huge bluffs I had been so impressed by. Even from my new vantage point they looked menacing. I could see the windswept upper reaches jutting out majestically over the valley below. As I surveyed the approaches I noticed there was quite possibly a way of climbing up and around the side of the mountain to the top of the bluffs. I resolved never to go there.

I turned and walked up onto a small plateau and found the track led into a narrow but very rocky, steep and dry creek bed. There was absolutely nowhere else to go considering the sides of the creek were burdened with vegetation so I began to walk up the centre of it. It was hot work but I made good progress. The creek was dry but totally clear of vegetation, making it obvious that at times a considerable amount of water must roar down it.

I continued stepping from rock to rock and soon passed another pole that confirmed I was on the right track. After puffing up a particularly steep section I looked up and noticed a flat area ahead and a clear sky in the background. I was definitely approaching a pass. I began to get excited. I quickened my pace ever so slightly before I remembered that rushing was not my style and I eased up.

Suddenly I saw the roof of a hut at the top of the pass. I was ecstatic and rushed on in gleeful abandon, almost skipping up the short winding track that led through the tussock to the hut. I had made it to halfway.

Chapter 13

Mind Games

Goat Pass Hut was a welcome sight. It sat in the midday sun, nestled on a sheltered plateau of tussock, flax and small alpine shrubs just short of the top of the pass. The hut was a wooden structure with a tin roof and a narrow veranda that ran the length of the northern side.

I exchanged pleasantries with some of the race officials checking off competitors as they passed by. I was offered water and used the opportunity as an excuse to stop and look around.

The view north from the hut was spectacular and took in the huge amphitheatre-like valley. It was here that the snow became trickles that became streams and gathered to form the headwaters of the Deception River. The end of the valley was ringed by a number of high peaks whose tussock approaches gave way to slopes of shattered rock that looked steep and uninviting.

To the west were the mighty bluffs and steep slopes flanking the valley I had made my way up. To the south and behind the hut were a series of rugged, fractured, tussock- and rock-covered alpine ridges that morphed into the forbidding mountains beyond. I was amazed at the area's harsh beauty. Although I have lived most of my life within a few hours' drive of some of the world's last truly beautiful and unspoiled wilderness areas I had never been this close before. I was awestruck. This was the stuff of postcards and I resolved to return one day.

I finished my drink and reluctantly moved on. Beyond the hut to the east and in the direction I wanted to go the track snaked its way to the right up a series of wooden steps before cutting back left and up to the top of the pass proper. I looked up to where the track disappeared and hoped it would be the last time I had to climb anything for the rest of my life. As I started out the Deception side of the pass had one final surprise for me. I ran from the hut and took the obvious path, straight to the toilet. I glanced back at two women sitting on the hut veranda and matched their grins at my minor embarrassment, grateful that no one else had seen it.

Goat Pass, at 1,070 metres, is the highest point on the course. I momentarily exulted in the fact that the course was all downhill from this point and cheerfully strode off, each step making a comforting 'tonk' sound as I made my way across the boardwalk. An elaborate system of boardwalks extends from the top of the pass to quite some way down the eastern side, designed and built at the bequest of the Department of Conservation to protect the fragile flora from boots and shoes. The boardwalks also kept all the traffic in one place. They were impressive little structures and as I surveyed my surroundings I appreciated the need for them. Although the area was currently dry, the soft voluminous islands of moss amongst a sea of even softer-looking mud suggested that the simple addition of even a small amount of water would result in drastic change.

While it was nice to see that someone had the foresight to ensure boardwalks were present to protect the environment from humans (and maybe humans from the environment) I was grateful for the boardwalks for other reasons. After all the ankle-twisting and rock-hopping and after trudging through smelly mud and freezing water, the boardwalk was running heaven. Not only was I running slightly downhill but I was doing so on a nice smooth surface devoid of mud, water, nasty scratchy bushes and other unpleasant aspects of an outdoor type.

I felt largely recovered from the previous few hours' running – as if it had never happened – and whizzed along elated. It was hard not to feel positive. I even felt as if I had a spring in my step. I tried to put a bit more effort into the springing up from a step and the boardwalk responded ever so slightly. It was bizarre. I actually had a spring in my step from the boardwalk.

I continued to trot along merrily until an errant thought popped into my head. It was a most unwelcome thought. I knew it would cause me trouble the moment I was aware I'd formed it. But now it was too late.

What would happen if one of the boards broke? Considering the staggering amount of moisture that each board undoubtedly had to absorb over the long winter months it was a wonder they weren't as soft as sponge. I continued to run but my confidence was seeping away. I began to cautiously appraise the boards ahead of me. I thought that if a board did break I would have absolutely no warning. My leg would drop through to the ground and snap like a twig under the stress of my forward momentum. It was a horrifying thought.

I carried on running but gave myself a stern talking-to.

I told myself it would be fine and to get a grip. Surprisingly it seemed to work and my confidence began to return. I would probably have dismissed my fear altogether if it had not been for one small undeniable fact. I came across a broken board.

I slowed considerably. I became tentative. I lost faith in the boards. I began to step cautiously over any board that looked even slightly off colour. The reassuring tonk, tonk, tonk that had accompanied each step before gave way to the sound of nervous shuffling feet. Fear was choking my progress.

It wasn't the first time.

In fact, fear of the unknown and incredibly unlikely had plagued me for years. Years of what a scientist might call 'baseless concern about statistical improbabilities'. This is where you take almost any task and somehow find within it some fear that you can magnify out of all proportion so that in the end you don't do what you wanted to do in the first place.

For example I am afraid to swim in deep water where I cannot see the bottom: because I can't see the bottom I cannot entirely dismiss from my mind the possibility (however remote) that Jaws is happily lurking out of sight and waiting for an opportune time to start tearing me to pieces. And I remember as a child not wanting to go to an island that had a tidal access road because I feared the tide would come up and stop us getting home. My companions eventually gave up trying to explain and left without me. Fear had cost me a great day with my friends.

For many years I thought that being fearful was synonymous with being sensible but now I realise that this is simply not true. Fear paralyses and obstructs. It can kill our dreams and shatter our hopes. It can stop us from even trying. It can cheat us of fulfilment. Fear so often stopped me doing what I wanted to do that one day I finally got sick of it and began to rebel. And I resolved to fight it more often.

Now in this uncertain moment I chose to fight. I changed my mindset.

I began a positive analysis. I reminded myself that I had overcome many fears to get to the Coast to Coast start line in the first place. I had survived the race so far. I was determined to get to the finish.

I perked up. So what if I broke my leg? At the very least I would have a fantastic story to tell and I might even get a ride in a helicopter.

I gritted my teeth and began to run again. As I built up confidence and speed I began to feel better. I did however make one small compromise: I ran on the side of the boards near the supports. It seemed like a sensible idea.

I was soon back up to full speed and making alarming progress down the mountain. I flew past a couple of other runners, flailing my arms about in a most undignified manner in an attempt to keep balance. I was barely in control as I raced down the track. While my weight may have been a disadvantage when going uphill, going down it was clearly an asset. Stopping was another matter.

As the steepness of the slope increased so did my speed and the need for caution. From time to time a series of steps would suddenly appear in front of me, necessitating a very quick decision. If there were only a few steps I would attempt to leap over the lot arriving at the bottom with only my knees separating the full crushing weight of my body from splattering on the boardwalk. If there were too many steps to jump I would try desperately to slow down with a series of quicker stutter steps accompanied by even more arm flailing and if possible a violent grab at any handy greenery. Somehow it all worked and I made some serious progress in a very short time.

The only hiccup happened when I came over the brow of a small rise and was confronted with a temporary end to the boardwalks and in their place a section of track. As I slowed with much arm flailing and stutter stepping I stood on some loose gravel and ended up on my backside. Despite this jolt I was having the time of my life.

I was back on my feet in a second and careering off over the rocks again, and before I knew it I was back on boardwalks and nearing the bottom of the hill.

I soon came to a series of short steep sections where the boardwalks gave way to oddly-spaced wooden-encased dirt steps. They were spaced in such a way that to maintain my pace I had to take a sort of giant lunge from one step to the next. It was a tremendous strain on my already tired thigh muscles.

I half-fell down the last few steps and glanced up to be confronted for the first time by the Mingha River. It was barely distinguishable from the Deception River on the other side of Goat Pass. Crisp clear water threaded its way through numerous rocks on its way down the valley. The only difference was that as a result of the more gradual loss of height the Mingha seemed to harmlessly gurgle away to itself rather than roar down the mountain like a runaway express train through a giant boulder slalom course. It certainly looked easier to cross and so I did – quickly. I scrambled up the other side and started to jog again.

A few minutes later I found myself in a portion of track with a series of tricky little sharp rocks. They jutted menacingly out of the soil, some reaching up to shin height and necessitating considerable care as I picked my way through. After a scary stumble I decided to walk through the rest of the section and even took a few moments to look around. To my left I noticed an impressive waterfall – just the sort of thing you have a tendency to miss when you are rushing along, eyes fixed on the ground as you scan it, hoping to spot in advance the next ankle-breaking obstacle.

The waterfall was high above me and I assumed from a quick look at a map of the area that it originated from Lake Mavis, a small alpine lake on the side of Mount Oates. At 2,008 metres Mount Oates, with its hidden lake and gnarled, rocky summit, presided over the left-hand side of the Mingha Valley.

With some sections of the track on boardwalks and others over a soft cushion of leaves, one could be forgiven for being lulled into overconfidence but a glance at the surrounding peaks reminded me this was the wilderness.

I dropped down a short distance onto more boardwalks. After the last few minutes of ups and downs the boardwalks were welcome relief. They were new and looked sturdy. I trotted along happily.

As I passed through the very wet and swampy section each step was accompanied by a 'squish' of water and the boardwalks seemed to bounce in response to every step.

A few minutes later and the track had changed again. Now I was running through a deeply rutted section under the canopy of a small stand of beech trees and had the dubious joy of trying to run across tree roots. This was no mean feat. While the track wound its way between the trees it was clear that over time foot traffic had eroded much of the soil, leaving bare tree roots above the ground. As though I was running across a series of used car tyres on a confidence course, I stepped carefully from one root to the next, trying to land solidly in the middle of each. It was treacherous going and I took great care. In one particularly shaded area the roots were damp and small pools of muddy slush had formed between them. There was no way I could run, even walking was slow.

I came out of the trees and hoped there weren't too many more sections like that. Looking ahead the ground was opening up and I could hear the gurgle of the river coming back on my left. I ran on. The track approached the river then turned sharp left to follow it downstream. The surface was now rutted with a gravel base and surrounded by native grasses. At times it was difficult to see the track at all and taking the next step became a leap of faith. Somehow I managed to get along safely. I noticed a small stream weaving in and around the track had dug out deep holes in different places. These holes became deeper and deeper until I came across a 20-metre section of track where the holes connected into a long trench that crossed the track three or four times. So well hidden by the native grass was the trench that I couldn't help but be impressed. Nature had created the perfect booby trap. It was a leg breaker for sure. It was as if nature was saying 'Hey, you people think you're so smart, try running across this in a hurry.' I had no interest in taking up the challenge and walked cautiously, stepping only where it was obvious others had stepped before me.

When I thought I had passed the worst of it I came across another competitor who appeared to be resting, sitting on a log beside the track and searching through his bag. I walked up and was about to grunt a greeting when I noticed he had a nasty gash just below his kneecap. Dark red blood oozed out of it and down the front of his leg. It looked deep. I was quite taken aback.

Not wanting to worsen his situation or shock him further I stayed calm. Well, almost.

'Bloody hell, are you okay? That looks terrible! Are you in pain? Can I do anything to help?'

Without looking up he grinned and continued to look through his small waist bag for what I assumed must be a bandage.

'Yeah, probably looks worse than it is. I'm fine really. I'll just bandage it up and walk out. You go ahead.'

I looked at him incredulously. To my mind he had a cut that had helicopter ride written all over it and here he was talking about walking out. I figured he was either incredibly brave or plain stupid.

He didn't look stupid.

Whatever he was he certainly knew his first aid. He deftly cleaned the cut and placed a small pad on it. He then produced a bandage and began wrapping it over the pad and around his leg with great skill. I was impressed. He looked up at me and smiled as I stood there gaping in awe and I instantly felt embarrassed at my squeamishness and decided to move on.

I wandered along the track that was now winding its way up and down beside the river. At times I was high above the river and on what was often a perilously narrow section of track yet I was lost in thought and oblivious to the danger.

I was thinking about the guy with the cut. How was it that some people seem so calm and casual about injury? How do they get like that? To me it looked for all intents and purposes like a serious injury. I had seen people pass out at the sight of far less, and yet Superman back there on the track was behaving as though he had simply dropped a piece of buttered toast on his leg.

His lack of concern, the way he dealt with the wound and the simple acceptance of his predicament impressed me. It was emotional control. There was no hysteria, just a cool clinical response to a problem.

When I was a young lad we had English neighbours whose mother tended to over-react to minor medical events. When one of the children hurt themselves and perhaps required a piece of sticking plaster (and this happened way too often) she would routinely call an ambulance. This was usually accompanied with a hell of a lot of shouting and screaming. We called her 'Mrs Psycho'.

God help you if you spilt the blood of any of the young Psychos. After I hit one of them in the face with a tennis ball one day I immediately bolted for home. I knew I had about five seconds to get off their property before she came for me.

The young Psychos themselves seemed very fragile. As opponents in a game of rugby they were like ripe tomatoes. If you tackled them they split and then they screamed. I've known babies that were tougher than those kids.

The only time one of them actually did get hurt their mum never found out about it. My brother and one of the young Psychos collided head-on while running around the house in opposite directions. It sounded like two bricks being clapped together. My brother was momentarily stunned but the other kid was out cold. After he came to, we kept him out of sight and bribed him with lollies until he was well enough to stagger home. We played around home for the next few days just in case we got asked any awkward questions.

Now don't get me wrong. I liked those kids a lot, but in those days their behaviour was not the norm for young Kiwi boys. In fact it was far from it. New Zealanders have tended to pride themselves on their stoicism. It is less obvious now, but a few decades ago displays of emotion either in celebration or pain were not encouraged. Once upon a time if a rugby player scored the winning try in the most important game of the year witnessed by fifty thousand delirious fans he got up and trotted back into position as if he'd simply run down that end of the field to check the length of the grass. Any other response would have seen him labelled over-exuberant. This was of course completely ridiculous behaviour but reflected the mood at the time. The message was clear. Overt displays of emotion were not encouraged. The New Zealand male was supposed to endure all and conquer all without any outward appearance of either pain or celebration.

When you compare this behaviour to the 'split-and-scream' response of the Psycho kids you can understand why none of the neighbourhood kids wanted to play with them. That is, all the neighbourhood kids except us. Since we lived next door to them our parents considered that in the spirit of neighbourliness we should.

Back on the track, my thoughts continued to swirl around in my head. I thought about the guy with the cut knee, the Psycho kids, the long-suffering Mrs Psycho, the hard men of rugby and how much New Zealand had changed over the years.

My mind was moving onto autopilot. Soon I had successfully slipped into a state where my conscious mind was focused well away from my physical state. I ran with almost total impunity to discomfort. I felt great.

Unaware of how tired I really was, I ran on and on. My thoughts slowly switched from the past to the present and then to my surroundings. I'm not quite sure what was so special about that moment but all of a sudden I became acutely aware of the quiet beauty around me. I quite happily jogged along the peaceful, well-worn track as it wound its way along the damp forest floor. I cruised up gentle rises and trotted down the other side. I came across small gurgling streams of amazingly clear, fresh water and with cupped hands scooped up a mouthful as I passed.

I saw no one. I heard no one. The only sounds were the distant songs of birds and my own footfalls. I was alone and at peace with the world.

I ran on. The bush was cool and largely sheltered from the glare of the sun. Patches of sunlight lit up sections of the forest floor and they stood out like bright silver beacons in a sea of green.

I sailed on through.

There were times when I was forced to skirt around the edge of significant bogs where it seemed an excellent place to put a boardwalk and yet there was none. At other times I ran high off the ground on narrow boardwalks where it seemed to me there was no need for them. Indeed, running on the soft moss below would have been like treading on the most lush green carpet imaginable.

But in my tired state I had forgotten what this area was about. The comfort of the visitor was not the priority. It was about protecting the whole beautiful and unique environment – preserving it for the future. It was about securing the opportunity for future generations to share in the wonder. It was about making sure that for the next hundred years and beyond thousands of soft city boys like me could wander off into the hills and see lush, soft green moss the way God intended. From two feet above it on a boardwalk!

Then I knew I was having a religious experience because in that moment I felt pride in the Department of Conservation. Just briefly I understood something of them and the way they see the land. For a second I could see past the over-zealousness and the bureaucracy and identify with the people and their passion for this wondrous land and I was grateful. I was grateful for the politicians who saw the need for a Department of Conservation. I was grateful for the Department and its staff who tended the land (even those who thought they owned it).

But before I started hugging trees and talking to rocks an unwelcome visitor began to slowly draw my mind away from my world of love and happiness, and back to reality.

It was discomfort. I catalogued my misery. My feet were sore. The constant changes of surface twisted them this way and that and they felt as if they had been subjected to a violent four-hour massage. I was pretty sure I had a couple of blisters. My knees ached, my hamstrings felt tight and I had been scratched in numerous places. I was chafing between the legs and my lower back felt uncomfortable every time I walked up a hill of any sort. I became aware that I was very tired and I began to wonder if the run would ever end.

No matter how much I tried to return to the happy cocoon-like state I had been in before, I could not. I was stuck in reality and forced to confront the discomfort.

Chapter 14

Suffering

I crossed a small stream and climbed up the steep bank on the other side. The effort made my thighs burn and left me short of breath. I noticed the ground ahead continued to slope upwards and realised I had most likely arrived at the base of Dudley Knob. I had heard from others that this small hill was the last climb on the course. This far into the journey it was the last thing I needed.

I reached the start of a steep slope and began to climb. With hands on knees, head low, back aching and looking far more like a caveman than I cared to imagine I made steady progress until my thighs began to protest and the burning sensation returned. I stopped to recover and looked around. I was halfway to the top. The track continued to climb ahead and then sidled up and across the slope over bare rock and sun-bleached gravel. It looked awfully hot up ahead.

With sweat pouring off me and my chest heaving with the effort I continued until I could see the top. Instead of slowing I charged up the last few metres to the top and stood there in the heat panting like a dog. I had made it.

Dudley Knob was nothing special. It was no more than a rocky outcrop at the end of a ridge that trailed down from the range of peaks away to my right. At the top where I stood there was a scattering of short trees and shrubs and this allowed views in most directions.

The view back up the Mingha Valley was magnificent. In the distance Mount Oates stood majestically overlooking the whole valley, and on its lower slopes I could almost see Goat Pass. It seemed so far away yet it had probably only taken an hour or so to get this far. The foreground between Goat Pass and where I stood was awash with lush green native forest.

Anxious to keep moving, I turned and carried on. I was surprised to find that I had not actually reached the highest point on Dudley Knob. The track led off towards another series of small rises before disappearing out of sight altogether. I resumed the grunting caveman posture I had perfected for uphill struggles and staggered along. I knew I must be an ugly sight but there was no place here for pride. That would come later when it was all over. The present was only for suffering.

At the point where I probably looked most ragged and entirely undignified a race photographer appeared and with a cheerful 'smile' took my picture. I mumbled 'bastard' as I passed and he grinned even wider. Here was a man enjoying his work.

As I climbed up another rise I caught a glimpse through the shrubs and head-high trees of the Mingha Valley stretched out before me. In the distance I thought I could make out where the run would finish. I recognised the distinctive bush-clad knob at the bottom of a distant ridge line as it came down to meet the river from the mountains off to the right. While it still looked some way off it seemed closer than the slopes of Mount Oates, where I had been less than an hour before. As I began my way down toward the river the thought that I might actually be near the end of the run gave my spirits a mighty lift.

There is something special about the first few minutes of running downhill after the effort of trudging uphill for any length of time. For a start it is just so easy. You simply lean forward and in no time you are taking giant strides and chewing up the miles. The fact that your heart was almost exploding out of your chest a few moments before on the uphill section is completely forgotten. Downhill running is different. You begin to think that perhaps you underestimated your ability, that you are fitter than you first thought, and you may even begin to feel cocky and self-assured.

None of this lasts long. In no time the honeymoon is over and your leg muscles are screaming for mercy as they try to slow you down. You begin to feel like a runaway freight train and it takes all your energy just to keep yourself at a manageable speed. Ten minutes before you might have been close to tears going uphill and vowing you would never go up another hill as long as you live, but now all you can think of is the pleasure of flat ground or a nice hill to walk up.

This is how I felt about five minutes after beginning my descent from

Rocks, scrub and cold mountain streams. The warm sunlight makes it a perfect day for adventure in the mountains. Paul's Camera Shop

Dudley Knob. I thundered headlong down the track, eyes anxiously searching ahead for safe passage through the rocks and any other obstacle that might cause my demise. I tried stutter steps and leaps to slow my progress but to no avail. My thighs were the only brakes I possessed and they were soon overused.

Remembering my descent from Goat Pass, I grabbed at a bush in an attempt to reduce my speed but tore most of it out of the ground. Next I grabbed at a small tree but it didn't slow my progress either: I only succeeded in hauling it out roots and all. I was a one-man environmental disaster. I felt terribly guilty. Then I caught a glimpse of the river through the trees. It was nearly over.

A minute or so later I came around a corner, belted across a small flat area and slowly chugged to a walk on a small rise next to the river. I was down.

I stopped running altogether and walked for a minute to catch my breath but mostly for the pure joy of having control over my forward momentum. Before long another runner passed me and I broke back into an uncomfortable trot.

I continued alongside the river, in the shade of the trees, before breaking out into the sunlight. After the relative dark of the bush the brightness of full sunlight and the glare off the river stones seemed incredible and my eyes took a while to adjust.

Looking up ahead, the river curved away from me to the left to a point where it met a ridge coming down from the right. I felt as if I was running around the edge of a small stony bay as I made my way towards the end of the ridge about 200 metres ahead.

For the first time in quite a while I noticed other runners ahead. Those that were closest to me didn't look in any better shape than me. They appeared to be running quite slowly, hunched over with heads down as they shuffled onwards. I knew how they felt.

As I approached the point where the ridge met the river I watched a small group of runners ahead of me. Two at the rear of the group, unnoticed by the others, veered off towards the water and the small bluff that marked the end of the ridge. They jumped into the river and swam a couple of strokes across a small pool at the base of the bluff before disappearing out of sight around the other side. I imagined they would be up and running again a few seconds later.

The fact that they had not hesitated at all told me they had been that way before. I looked back to watch the three runners that had chosen the ridge over the water. They were still no more than halfway up what I guessed to be a 10-metre climb. In light of the fact they still had to climb down the other side as well I made up my mind to try the river. Anyway, it was hot and the refreshingly cool water was certainly more inviting than another climb.

A minute later I arrived at the water's edge and with the confidence of one who follows I jumped in with barely a second thought. The cold water gripped me. Even though my head never went under I gasped for air. My heart went crazy. First it nearly stopped when I hit the water then it started beating at the rate of a hummingbird's. I swam a few strokes then dog-paddled into the shallow water until my feet touched the ground. As soon as they did I launched myself out of the water. I felt more like I had been electrocuted than been for a short swim in a river. For the next two minutes I felt extremely alert!

I flew across the stones beside the river and almost immediately caught up with the three runners who had climbed over the ridge. I passed them as if they were standing still. I roared across the next river crossing, passing two more runners. I was on fire.

But it didn't last. As the shock of the cold water wore off, the weight of my wet clothes became apparent and an almost overwhelming feeling of tiredness took hold. My pace slowed dramatically and I dawdled along as best I could.

Looking ahead, I figured I now only had a few kilometres to go at worst. But it looked tough. Stretched out before me lay the river stones of the Mingha Valley, while just above them the heat haze shimmered menacingly in the distance. I could now also see lots of other runners stretched before me as they fought their own way to the finish over the loose stones of the riverbed.

I looked at the ground as I ran. The rocks and stones themselves varied in size from about that of a tennis ball up to the size of a basketball. Running on them was awkward and energy-sapping work. It wasn't too difficult running on the flat, smoother sections with smaller stones. There was the faint outline of a track to follow and initially at least, a lot of the ground

Keeping my balance. Tired muscles work overtime as the real suffering begins.
Paul's Camera Shop

was firm. However, every now and again, without warning, I came across a section where the stones were loose and had a lot of give underneath. It was like going from sealed road to soft sand. Every step was tiring.

At other times on the bigger rocks I tried to hop from one rock to the next rather than thread my way between them. While this technique was faster, the constant leaping from here to there all the time was incredibly hard work.

I also had to make decisions about the relative safety of landing on the next rock while in the midst of a leap. I would think the rock was suitable as I leapt toward it, only to see as I stretched out to land on it that it was half the width I had thought it was. Others moved as I took off or landed, which did nothing for my confidence.

With every leap, every misplaced step, every wobble and correction, every slip, every loss of traction I became more and more tired. Not only did I feel it physically but also mentally, and as time wore on it became harder and harder to keep going.

Up until now the journey had been interesting. But I was now at a point in the run where nothing mattered to me but that each painful step was closer to the point where I could stop. I didn't give a damn for the view, the vegetation or the wildlife.

Other runners were now no distraction or comfort either. I had no desire to talk to anyone. All I wanted to do was stop. So I did. I slowed to a walk for about 20 seconds before I decided two things. Firstly, if I walked it was going to take me longer till I could stop, and secondly, I was not going to give up and walk. It was bloody uncomfortable to run but it wasn't impossible and so if I continued to walk I would be giving up, admitting defeat. I wasn't ready to do this. While I was running I was doing my best. If I stopped and walked I was not. I wanted to look back and be proud of myself.

Slowly I lurched forward and began to jog again. A surge of pride filled my chest and I felt a lift. I realised I was learning about myself. Yes, I was suffering physically like I had never suffered before but despite the incredible level of discomfort my mind was still running the show. It occurred to me that once the decisions were made my body would follow. I also realised that as long as a flicker of desire remained I would be able to keep going.

So I began to focus on it. The Finish. I wanted it. I wanted it badly. I wanted to feel the victory. It was the only thing keeping me going.

It struck me that above all I possessed the desire to keep going that was going to get me to the finish. This gave me comfort. I was winning the most important battle of the day, the battle in my mind.

As I suffered across the rocky plain a helicopter flew over and buzzed around me for a while like an oversized gnat. Through the maelstrom of rotor-frenzied dust-laden wind I glanced up at a cameraman as he aimed at me in my misery. I was tempted to give him a one-fingered salute but couldn't spare the energy.

How dare he chronicle my pain? It was mine and mine alone. I lowered my head and carried on. I ran on the loose rocks and stones. I ran on the soft gravel. I felt like crying. I ran through more water. It was cold and refreshing but it was only temporary relief. I still was not at the finish.

I ran on. I tripped and fell and grazed my palms. It hurt. I got up slowly and began to run again. I wanted to stop. But I didn't. I kept running. I was in my own little selfish insular world of pain and suffering where nothing mattered but me and my pain.

I ran toward a raised bank where I could see people. To the right was another raised bank that I saw supported a set of railway tracks. It couldn't be far to go now. As I reached the people I realised this was not the finish. My heart sank but my head made me run on.

The spectators sat and stood about in a hushed manner looking for those they knew. They said nothing. They knew there was nothing they could say to ease the pain so they clapped in quiet reverence as we passed by.

I ran along the raised bank in a daze. Another runner loomed up beside me wearing a yellow cap. We eyeballed each other but said nothing. The crunch of our footfalls on the gravel set a simple rhythm. We ran side by side and stride for stride. The sound and the presence of the other runner gave me energy. It was as if somehow running side by side, stride for stride, we shared the load. I can't explain why but its effect on me was undeniable. I felt better. I felt stronger. A few minutes later we reached the end of the raised bank. I could see up ahead about one and a half kilometres away in the distance a large and colourful group of people strewn all over a river stopbank watching and waiting for runners. I knew this must be Klondyke Corner and the finish of the run.

I could see also that I had to make a choice. There were two ways to get there. One was to cross the railway line that was now around in front of me, then run down its bank and begin a long and difficult route over a sea of river rocks and stones. This way I would probably have to cross the river twice as it weaved back and forth. It looked like hot, hard work.

The alternative route was to follow the railway line out to the left and cross the rail bridge to the other side of the river. From there I could run down the bank and along what looked like a faint four-wheel-drive track near the edge of the river rocks and stones. It looked longer but the running looked easier.

The guy in the yellow cap went straight down the bank and started the direct route across the rocks. For a brief second I was tempted to go with him for the company but I desperately wanted the easier route. I turned to cross the rail bridge. As I did I scanned the track into the distance for the slightest sign of any train. The thought of trying to get across the narrow bridge with a massive coal train bearing down on me was frightening. Seeing none I set off.

I dragged myself across the bridge. I was exhausted. At the far end, relieved to get off the rail tracks, I slid carefully down the bank, my legs protesting all the way. I looked about for the track I had seen. It was difficult to find in the long dry grass but I stumbled across it a few seconds later. With a sigh I jogged slowly onto it and began to make my way along. I knew I had made the right decision. The track was firm and certainly looked a lot easier to run on than the river rocks only a few metres away.

I glanced across the river for the guy in the yellow cap. He was a few hundred metres off to my right and still ahead of me, but struggling. His progress seemed slow and he stumbled twice in the few moments I watched him. A few minutes later I looked again. I was in front. Not that I cared any for competition. I had left it far behind. There were no rivals now, only comrades in suffering. Observations of fellow athletes served only to compare route choice. My sole purpose in life now was to get to the finish and stop running. There was nothing else.

I watched as the bright colours of the crowd got closer and closer. They fixated me. My salvation lay amongst them.

I left the comfort of the track to cross the river stones for the last time. I had less co-ordination on the rocks than before and stumbled often. Once I tripped and fell. The sharp pain from my already grazed palms reminded me to make more effort to lift my feet.

I noticed a few runners just ahead. They had obviously taken the same path over the rail bridge. Beyond them was another line of runners coming from the left and merging at the riverbank. These had taken the more direct route. I looked back down the line of runners for the chap with the yellow cap. He was well back. I would be the first to rest.

I was so close to the spectators I could make out individuals on the bank as they awaited runners. I could see people clapping as each runner came up to the bank, climbed it and disappeared over the other side.

Almost at the same time I came across the river. I jogged down to the water's edge and became self-conscious as I noticed just how many people were scattered about waiting for runners. I crossed carefully not wanting to fall and embarrass myself. I needn't have worried. The crowd of onlookers clapped as they did with each runner. Quite unexpectedly a surge of immense pride and satisfaction welled up within me. It had been such a long way and now I was nearly there.

I began to feel energised. It seemed very odd. A few minutes before I was at death's door and now within sight of the finish and with a few people clapping I found energy I had no idea existed. Was I that shallow? Was that all it took to take me from death's door to recovery? I decided I didn't care. I took it for what it was, sustenance to help me finish.

I charged the last few metres to the riverbank and hauled myself up and over it. I staggered down the other side and found myself in a large finishing chute fenced off with bright orange tape.

Down the far end and waiting under the finishing banner was Robin Judkins. Running like an arthritic seventy-year-old, I tottered across the grass to where he stood under the banner and then quite wonderfully I stopped running.

He shook my hand. 'Well done, welcome to Klondyke Corner.' I wanted to speak but nothing came out of my mouth. I walked through the finish area, grinned at my friends, found a vacant patch of grass and collapsed to the ground. I lay there on my back in peace and contentment with my eyes shut and sunlight warm on my face.

Chapter 15

Klondyke

Klondyke Corner was alive. Most of the year this tiny place is no more than a quiet rest stop with a couple of wasp-infested toilets and an open-sided day shelter. However, for one night each year it becomes the campsite and focal point for over a thousand people. Tents, caravans, cars and people were everywhere.

The area designated for camping was a hub of ceaseless activity. Friends and acquaintances were camped together in small groups. They scurried around their sites busily repairing equipment, pumping up tires, preparing food and fussing over their athletes, some of whom had only recently finished. Laughter and excitement filled the air as everyone talked about the day's adventures. The athletes recounted the highs and lows of their journey while support crews told of their frantic attempts to get this and that ready: all that had occurred behind the scenes in the absence of their athlete.

Most of the action was over by the finishing chute. From early afternoon a constant stream of runners appeared over the stopbank and staggered to the finish, cheered on by the crowd. As soon as their race number was visible the witty announcer, the newspaper columnist Joe Bennett, yelled their name and made some comment.

'Here comes number 747, keep on Boeing!'

'Now what have we here, it's number 645: a father of 3 from Wellington.'

Once they crossed the line friends and supporters often enveloped them before leading them away to a seat, food and whatever else their hearts desired. Some collapsed and were dragged off to the medical tent followed by a concerned band of friends and relatives. Others walked away in a painful-looking bow-legged fashion, not unlike a child with a full nappy. No doubt suffering the effects of chafing. Still others wept in pain or ecstasy or both while their friends and relatives wept along with them. The emotion was catching. The whole blubbering band would move off together, some hugging and others arm-in-arm, leaving those around them to ponder the significance of the athlete's effort.

Behind the finishing area were a number of stalls and shops where sponsors of this and that were selling bikes, kayaks, energy supplements and clothing. Some vendors were selling food at the sort of outrageous prices you could only charge in the middle of nowhere. Despite this there were long lines of people willing to pay. The beer tent was doing brisk business and all around athletes and crews sat about sipping ice-cold beer and enjoying the sun. There was even a band playing live music, although in my opinion describing the sounds they made as music is being rather generous. They were clearly enjoying themselves though and no one seemed to mind.

Not far from the band was a huge marquee where the soothing caresses of masseurs tended the bodies of tired athletes. The unmistakable smell of massage oil was thick in the air. Athletes staggered in to the marquee, slumped on beds, lay there unmoving for 20 minutes then gingerly got off the bed and with a grimace thanked their masseurs and staggered off. It was an often-repeated cycle.

As the afternoon progressed the number of finishing athletes tapered off. The chute was empty for five or 10 minutes at a time. The officials wandered about and chatted amongst themselves and Judkins called for a seat. As the time between runners lengthened so did the magnitude and significance of their achievement. The crowd beside the chute began to swell as runners who had finished hours earlier came to salute those for whom the effort was so great.

A huge man appeared in the chute. He lumbered along with a tortured grin on his face, at somewhere between a walk and a jog. The announcer revealed he had lost 22 kilograms over the previous year just to get to the start of the race and the crowd went nuts.

Not long after came a man who had in the past year finally recovered from a long fight with cancer. He crossed the line and was immediately enveloped by his family in such a way that it was obvious what he meant to all of them. It was incredibly emotional and affected all those who witnessed it.

Part of the crowded scene at Klondyke Corner, where for one night each year more than a thousand people camp at the end of day one. Mark Elliott

The finish of the mountain run, Klondyke Corner. Announcer extraordinaire Joe Bennett prepares his next quip, while Robin Judkins (seated in chute) awaits the next runner. Mark Elliott

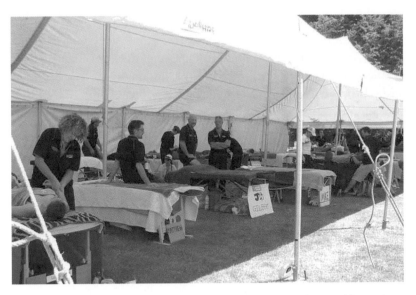

The massage tent handles the early arrivals, while those who need it most are still a long long way away. Mark Elliott

Sponsor tents and spectators out in the midday sun.Mark Elliott

Scenes like this occurred all afternoon.

Late in the day, as many were preparing food for their evening meal, the loudspeaker announced the imminent arrival of one of the last runners. People rushed from everywhere to line the finishing chute to welcome in a woman in her late fifties. She laboured the last few metres to the finish and into the waiting arms of her husband while the crowd clapped and shouted encouragement.

She wasn't the last, though. The last person to finish day one was a man from Nelson by the name of Jeff Moore. Jeff had no crowd to greet him when he crossed the line – the only people who witnessed his courageous feat were his support crew, family and the tail-end Charlies, officials whose job it was to see that all runners were safely off the course. You see, Jeff arrived around 12.30am after a two-and-a-half-hour bike ride followed by a fourteen-and-a-half-hour run. While his bike ride wasn't too bad his run was extremely slow. In fact his run was completed in the slowest time ever recorded. Still, not bad for a man with only one leg.

I awoke at some ungodly hour to the sound of car engines starting in the predawn. As I lay there warm in my sleeping bag, I listened to hushed voices outside in the cold, grateful that it wasn't me. Support crews all around our campsite were pulling down tents, hastily grabbing breakfast and making final preparations to kayaking equipment, before heading to the river. According to the programme support crews had to report to the kayak transition point at 5.30am so that each competitor's gear could have a complete safety check before use later that morning. Poor bastards.

I found my watch. It was 5am. I guesstimated I had had about six and a half hours' sleep and this after about four hours sleep the night before. I had spent much of the intervening time in considerable discomfort. At home I would have thought that I needed a good eight to nine hours, sleep a night just to function without wanting to maim most people I met. Here I was getting nowhere near that amount of sleep yet I felt fine. Not only that, my body felt pretty good as well. Most of the aches and pains from yesterday were a distant memory. Considering what I had been through I had recovered remarkably well. Within a few hours of finishing (after food and a warm shower) I had even contemplated the thought that I might like to run again, some day.

I found that incredible. Yesterday I would have accepted a cash offer for my legs. I wasn't ever intending to use them again. I would certainly never run again. Now I felt fine. The pain was fleeting. I had learnt another important lesson.

I lay for a while longer before I got bored and decided to make some breakfast. Although I wasn't feeling very hungry I knew that I must eat to provide energy for the day ahead. I laboured through cereal, fruit and toast but my heart just wasn't in it. I got into my gear and prepared my bike. I had a big day ahead.

Chapter 16

Crash

I stood holding my bike and shivering from a mixture of cold and pre-race nerves. It was shortly after 7am.

The first group of 10 to leave for the river were not scheduled to leave until 7.30am. Hundreds of other cyclists milled about in various states of readiness while officials checked the starting equipment and began to encourage competitors into their starting groups.

Looking around, I could see that the common plastic rubbish bag was clearly the most popular pre-race attire. It seemed like every second cyclist wore one over his or her cycling gear in an attempt to keep warm. They could then be disposed of just prior to the start. With most support crews already at the river there was no guarantee anything left at Klondyke would ever be seen again.

A stern woman with a clipboard went to the head of the column of gathering cyclists and took control.

'Right let's get started. Number 201?'

'Here.'

'202?'

Yes, I'm here.'

'203?'

'Yep,' said a cyclist just arriving.

'204?'

Silence. 'Number 204?' Nothing.

'Where the hell is 204?'

The lady with the checklist gave a deep sigh and cursed under her breath as she scanned the crowd for the missing cyclist. Realising she was wasting time she moved on.

'Number 205?

'Yes.'

'Number 206?'

'Yes, sir, ma'am,' was the loud military answer from the young man wearing 206. Without moving a single muscle in her face she lifted her eyes from the page to see his huge cheeky grin. She stared at him dispassionately for a few seconds before returning to the page.

'207?'

'Yep.'

'208?'

'Yes.'

'209?'

'Here.'

'Excuse me?'

'Yes.'

'I'm number 204 and I think I am in this group,' said a young woman meekly. The clipboard lady looked hard into the eyes of 204 for a few seconds before putting a tick on her clipboard and walking off without a word. Number 204 went quietly to her spot. This was repeated for over ten minutes before my own group's turn came.

'Come forward,' said the start marshal. Ten nervous cyclists shuffled forward. We stopped just short of the electronic timing mat that would record our departure time.

A young chap in his early twenties jostled his way nervously in beside me with a bike that looked as if it weighed as much as a piece of paper. Everything about him looked fast, from his shiny lycra to his aerodynamic helmet.

'30 seconds,' said the marshal.

I looked at my bike and hoped everything would be ok, then realised I had forgotten my water bottle. It was too late. 'Oh well,' I thought, 'it's only 15 kilometres.'

The marshal started a countdown. 'Five, four, three, two.' On 'one' we all lurched forward and were away.

Almost immediately the young chap was up and gone. I had no doubt he was chasing the group that had started one minute earlier, and I had even less doubt that he would catch them.

The rest of us cruised along comfortably together for a few minutes at a good pace. The fact we were travelling at a crisp 35 kilometres per hour without much effort meant that either over the last 12 hours I had miraculously become a much better cyclist, or we were going downhill. For a while either was a possibility but I soon realised we were in fact on a barely discernable downhill slope.

I was fourth in line and feeling quite comfortable as we began to cross a long one-lane bridge over the upper Waimakariri River. I looked down at the water below. It appeared shallow and tame and I hoped it would still be so 15 kilometres downstream when we got into our kayaks.

Once across the bridge we turned left and as we did so I glanced back to see there was no rider immediately behind me. I realised that four of us had broken away from the other five. 'Wow,' I thought, 'I have actually broken away from someone!' It was terribly exciting.

There was already quite a big gap between my group and the remaining five. I began to ponder more seriously the idea that perhaps I had improved since yesterday! Excited, I turned my attention back to my three companions. As we took turns at leading we all smiled smugly at each other. It was obvious we all felt good.

We continued to whizz along in unison and even charged up a small rise side by side. Things were looking good. We ploughed over the top of the rise and down the other side and began to take short turns at the front. It was fast and exciting and I was feeling more and more confident.

Just when I was sure that indeed I had magically transformed into a much better cyclist, a bigger group came whizzing past the four of us. There were nine of them including three women and most of them grinned happily as they swept past us, glorying in the triumph of the capture.

Our four joined on as the tail came past and we were now 13. While I was a trifle disappointed to have lost a minute to these nine so soon after the start, I was glad to be with a bigger group. It meant more cyclists to share the workload and at the same time lessened the chance of others catching us.

With such a short ride to the river and a bigger group to work with, the power was on. The front five riders drove hard and I knew there was little I could do but try and hang on for as long as possible. We roared along the road between large fields of grass and began to climb a gentle slope. As the pace eased the bunch closed up, I moved up a couple of places and began to look around at the surroundings. The mountains were magnificent and I stared up at them in awe. Despite the fact that it was high summer I could clearly see large patches of pure white snow glistening brightly in the early morning sunlight on the peaks above.

As we crested the top of the hill I could see the road stretched out before us. It wound its way over to the right-hand side of the valley and in the distance I could see it climbed a series of humps before disappearing around the side of the lower slopes of the mountains.

As we began our descent we passed a woman quietly riding on her own. Someone politely asked her if she wanted to join our train to the river but she declined. 'I don't do bunches,' she said. And with that we were gone. Her words rang in my ears and puzzled me. Why would she say she didn't do bunches?

We swept down the long descent and spread out slightly. It was nice to relax somewhat and catch my breath before the hills. Halfway down the slope and feeling confident I got into the tuck position I had tried for the first time the day before. I could feel the bike gathering speed as I lowered my profile to the wind. I slipped out to the side of the rider in front of me, intending to head toward the front of the bunch. Surprisingly I made almost no headway. I was puzzled momentarily until I suddenly noticed the front five riders were not only bent over in similar aerodynamic tuck positions as I was but they were also pedalling frantically. I couldn't match their speed. I went to slip back into line again but the gap had closed and I had lost my original place. I had to settle for second to last. It was to save my day.

At speed we belted down the last of the hill and on to a short flat section of road. Looking ahead I caught a glimpse past the rider in front of me to the start of another small hill. Just as I was thinking how I was enjoying the ride I heard in front of me a scream followed by the sickly sound of tangling metal scraping on coarse road chip.

In a millisecond I knew what was happening and thoughts came quickly.

Crash. High speed. Close together.

We're all going down.

Must escape. Get the brakes. Squeeze. Harder.

More screaming. I couldn't see past the rider directly in front of me but I could sense the pile-up approaching through his movement.

He's going. Escape left. Aim for the grass.

I turned sharp left in the same instant as the rider in front of me. His forward momentum suddenly stopped in the middle of his turn as he hit an unseen object. I smashed into him. We went over as if in slow motion and I landed on top of him and then something hit me and it was over.

I lay there stunned. Someone was groaning. The guy that had been last in line had landed on top of me. He got off and I stood up. I felt shaken but seemed to be unhurt. We had landed on the grass verge at the side of the road. Others weren't so lucky.

A woman lying on the road was crying. Beside her was a tangle of about five bikes. Other riders stood beside the wreckage in a stunned daze, some sporting cuts and grazes.

I picked up my bike. It looked OK. I didn't know what to do next. A rider walked past carefully nursing one of his hands and saying over and over again, 'Aaagh my wrist, my wrist'.

I became aware of an approaching cyclist. It was a woman riding on her own. I immediately recognised her as the woman we'd invited to join our bunch at the top of the last hill. She rode slowly past the chaotic scene with a look of absolute horror on her face. In that moment it dawned on me just why she had said she 'didn't do bunches'.

'If you're not hurt help someone who is,' said an older man who was helping the crying woman to her feet.

I looked around. No one looked as if they needed any more help than they were already receiving. The bloke who had landed on me looked at me then picked up his bike as well. 'Nothing to do here, let's go,' he said. I nodded.

I got on my bike. It felt different, like I had grabbed the wrong one. As I slowly pedalled off I began to examine it. The handlebars were slightly out of line and pointing to the left. There was nothing I could do to correct this while riding so I left them alone. I noticed the brake levers were also bent. The right one had taken the impact and had buckled off to one side. I tried to get it back into position and managed to partially succeed.

We started up the hill and I noticed for the first time that the calf muscle on my left leg was stiff and sore. It wasn't bad but it was there and I wondered if it might give me trouble later in the day.

I struggled up the hill alongside the other crash survivor but my heart wasn't in it and it wasn't long before other cyclists started coming past. A group of five eased past as we reached a plateau high above the river plain. They invited us to 'hop on' but we both politely declined. I would have ridden off the cliff rather than go anywhere in a bunch. I decided that I didn't do bunches anymore!

The rest of the ride passed without further incident. I was, however, a lot more tentative. I avoided other cyclists and on the downhills I kept my fingers hovering over the brakes like a trigger-happy soldier.

After a series of short, painful uphill and slow, cautious downhill sections I rounded a corner and looked ahead to see a small rise and a waiting crowd that marked the end of the bike section. I was greatly relieved. My bike was developing some strange sounds and I was starting to lose faith in its ability to get me further in one piece.

As I laboured up the last few metres of the rise two cyclists came flying past as if locked in a personal battle to the line. One of them had a race number exactly 70 numbers higher than mine. It was sobering stuff. His group had started seven minutes behind my group yet he had still managed to make up the deficit in only 15 kilometres. Even with the time I lost due to the bike crash I found the thought that he was so much quicker than I was quite depressing.

My bike shuddered to a halt and I leapt off. I had to run with it about a kilometre down a dirt road to the river and then kit up for the trip down the river.

After yesterday's effort a solitary kilometre down a gentle slope was little challenge and so as the co-ordination returned to my legs I began to enjoy myself. A little further on down the hill and I saw the whole transition area for the kayaking leg laid out before me. It was magnificent. For the first time I got a grasp of the scale of the event. Not far below, the Mount White bridge led across to the opposite bank of the Waimakariri where hundreds of support crews were waiting for their competitors. On the grassed area beside them row upon row of kayaks were laid out in numerical order. In neat little bundles beside each kayak were lifejackets, paddles, helmets and safety gear. Off in the distance and looking very strange in light of the surroundings, were masses of support vehicles. There were very orderly rows and rows of campervans, cars and trucks glistening in the early morning sun. It looked remarkably as though a supermarket car park had been magically transported onto a tussock-covered plain in the middle of nowhere.

I trotted down the last and steepest section of hill and at the bottom came across the main West Coast rail line. This would be my fourth crossing during the race. I leapt across it, grateful that there was no train to delay my progress. On a number of occasions cycle bunches had been split in two by the not-so-timely arrival of a train. The half that managed to get across before the train would congratulate themselves before charging off to maximise their advantage, while the other half waited impatiently hoping the train was a short one.

As I began to cross the bridge I saw an unmistakable figure in front of me. It was Mr Colossus. He took up half the bridge and was lumbering along with the intensity of a grazing cow. I immediately wondered what kind of watercraft he possibly hoped to caress down the river. Looking across the stones I half-expected to see a support crew of five or six men wrestling a pontoon with a sofa strapped on top to the water's edge while another two carried a giant paddle carved out of a small tree.

I jogged past him and nodded. He was the king of cyclists and I paid homage. He grinned back and I don't know why but I suddenly knew he was going to be a hell of a kayaker too.

I found Graham and Chris, who led me to my beloved Eclipse where I began to put on my kayak gear. I started with my helmet and then took it off when I discovered I couldn't pull my life-jacket over my head with it on. I was feeling nervous and edgy. I tried to relax but it was difficult, being so charged with adrenalin after the events of the morning ride.

Across the river a short, sharp and very loud horn blast announced the arrival of a big black empty coal train from the east coast as it returned west. It wound its way around the side of the hill immediately above the far riverbank. There was a minor panic as a couple more loud blasts on the horn scared everyone well clear of the tracks and satisfied the driver that those who hadn't gone deaf from the first blast surely would be now.

I turned back to my gear. With lifejacket and helmet already on I quickly put on the spray skirt and slopped some sunblock on my face and neck. I grabbed my kayak shoes and tried to put them on but my right foot wouldn't go completely into the shoe.

While I struggled with my shoes Mr Colossus was getting into his kayak. It wasn't the pontoon I had imagined but the next best thing: a very big and practical sea kayak. It couldn't have been more stable unless it had had an outrigger attached. It was a smart choice. He wasn't likely to fall out easily. His lifejacket looked big and practical too. In fact it was so big and puffy it looked like he had a couple of sleeping bags strapped around his chest. He got into his kayak with help from his crew and took off with a few violent slashes of his paddle. At the speed he left I doubted I would see him again. God help anyone who got in his way.

Anxious to get away myself I finally managed to ram my foot into the errant shoe and jumped to my feet. I rushed to get the rest of my gear on while the lads took the Eclipse to the water's edge. They held it for me while I finished a hell of a fight with a buckle on my lifejacket by conceding defeat and swearing at it. I couldn't believe it: gear that had given me no trouble all year was suddenly falling apart or getting tangled up. I couldn't put on a shoe, buckles wouldn't do up and I was doing everything in the wrong order. The lads noticed I was having trouble.

'Why don't you just try and relax,' said one of them as I headed toward the kayak. It was good advice: a kayak is not a place to be tensed up.

I got in and we clipped down the spray skirt. Graham passed me the paddle and with a quick word of thanks to the lads and few cautious paddle strokes I was off to face the river.

Chapter 17

River Antics

I paddled out into the river's main flow and started to pick up speed. I had heard that it was fairly tame for the first few kilometres and was thankful that I was going to have time to get my balance right before the horrors of the gorge, and warm to the task in front of me. Looking ahead I saw that the main flow of the water was split into two streams, or braids, and they seemed to part and come together at various points for as far as I could see.

I hadn't gone more than a hundred metres when I noticed a few problems. First, as soon as my hands got wet my paddle unexpectedly started slipping around in my hands and I felt like I was trying to hold an eel. Second, the trim on my boat was all wrong. The nose of the kayak was much higher out of the water than normal and it almost seemed like I was paddling uphill, if such a thing were possible.

I decided I had to deal with the paddle first. I wondered how on earth it could have got so slippery until I remembered the sunblock. I had rubbed it all over my face, neck and upper arms that morning. I examined my left palm and noticed a bead of water roll across it like a raindrop off the bonnet of a freshly waxed car. Oh, great – water-resistant sunblock. I had to get it off and I had to do it now or risk losing my grip on the paddle when it might be crucial.

I began to rub my hands on everything I could in an attempt to remove the sunblock. It wasn't as easy as it might sound. I used my sleeves, the lifejacket, the spray skirt and even the backs of my hands, but because the sunblock was water-resistant and my hands were already wet nothing short of sandpaper was going to get them completely back to normal. In the end I was left with an annoying slippery residue on my hands as testament to my lack of forethought and experience.

Next I had to clean the shaft of the paddle itself, so I pulled the sleeve of my polypropylene top down and vigorously attacked the parts of the paddle I routinely gripped. It seemed to work reasonably well and soon I was off again. However, from time to time I hit a rock or the bottom of the river with the paddle and without warning it would slip out of one or both of my hands and give me a heck of a fright.

I turned to the problem with the trim. Instead of being flat in the water, the nose of the kayak seemed about an inch higher than it should be. Instead of gliding over the top of the water the back half of the kayak was submerged enough to be pushing water before it. It was bloody annoying. To keep the boat moving the way it was would require considerably more energy than I had prepared to spend. I had to find out the reason for the imbalance, and quickly.

I puzzled over it. What the hell was going on? What had changed? I had all my survival gear stuffed in behind the seat but it was not heavy enough to raise the nose that much. And then it hit me. The drinking water. I remembered that the night before while preparing the kayak Graham and I had needed a space for the bag of survival gear. In an effort to make room we had pushed the four litres of flavoured drinking water further down toward the rear of the kayak. No doubt the extra weight had upset the delicate balance of the kayak and resulted in raising the nose. I felt like a complete idiot. The effect of the extra weight had never even occurred to me as I laboriously moved the water container back in the boat and taped it securely in place.

Now that I knew what the problem was, I paddled on angrily wondering what on earth I was going to do. The drink container was taped in with so much tape it would have taken five minutes and a hacksaw to get it out.

I felt even worse when I began to notice the occasional kayak coming past with a clear plastic tube taped to the side. These were set up so the kayaker could drink directly from the river. I was annoyed with myself. What had I been thinking? Here I was with four litres of drinking water in the back of my kayak forcing the nose up like the bow of the Titanic while all around me were millions of litres of clean fresh drinking water. All I needed for energy was a small amount of flavoured sugary concentrate. The rest I could have drawn from the river.

I had to act quickly. Two minutes later I had found an answer. To get the kayak back on even keel I was going to have to suck out a couple of litres of water from my supply and spit it out. It was my only sensible choice. I got started. For the next 15 minutes I paddled down the river sucking copious amounts of water out of my drink system and spitting it into the river. I got a few odd looks but I didn't care. All I wanted to do was get the kayak back on an even keel and make it easier to paddle. I would worry about looking normal after that.

Finally the nose of the kayak was down to an acceptable height and the boat moved over the water more gracefully. I was able to stop sucking water. It was a great relief. I hadn't figured that after 20 minutes of paddling the most tired muscles would be the ones all around my face!

At this point in the day it would have been easy to beat myself up for all the mistakes I had made. I decided to turn it around and focus on a few of the positive things I had achieved. This took a little longer than I anticipated but eventually I came up with a few thoughts. For one thing I had successfully solved the problems of the paddle and the trim without having to stop and secondly, in doing so, I had diverted my attention from the complexities of the river. I was so busy with my paddle and with spitting vast quantities of water back into the river that I didn't have time to worry about any of the first few tricky rapids. They had come and gone without incident. I figured it was all a matter of perspective.

Now that I had more control over the paddle and the boat on an even keel I finally had a chance to look around and relax. I was kayaking down one of a number of navigable braids that meandered in an easterly direction across the centre of a large, dry, grassy plain. It was high summer in the backcountry. The arid plain was surrounded by light-coloured foothills sporting dirty smudges where scrub and bush grew thickly in the gullies and creeks. Not far beyond and rising in the background the bush-clad mountains with their barren, jagged, rocky peaks stood majestically silent in the early morning light. I breathed a happy sigh. This is what I was here for: achievable adventure in the most beautiful country in the world.

On the river itself there were kayakers all around me – people of all shapes and sizes paddling a wondrous array of kayaks. I found their presence comforting. I felt that if I somehow happened to get into difficulty there would be plenty of help around. But I soon changed my mind.

As I paddled around the next bend I was confronted with a simple little rapid but with a small bend to navigate about halfway down. I watched fascinated as those in front of me began to go down it. A woman hit another boat and both spun out just in front of me. Another person seemed to lose balance halfway down the rapid and was soon upside down, while beyond him a man was doing a horrible job of emptying out a very new and impressive-looking boat. At that point I realised I was more likely surrounded by potential witnesses than rescuers. I had a fairly healthy suspicion that if I did get into difficulty the best my family could hope for would be a good description of how I met my end, rather than any tangible help.

Over the next few minutes the river veered left and soon I found myself paddling directly into the sunlight. I looked up to assess where I should go next and was struck by the beauty of the scene before me. Hundreds of kayakers were paddling into the low morning sunlight. Every time a paddle left the water the sun caught the brilliantly sparkling droplets as they flew off the blades like exploding fireworks. It was a magic sight.

The biggest explosions of sunlit water seemed to emanate from the paddle of a huge figure way ahead in the distance. There was only one person it could be. Mr Colossus was thrashing his way down the river looking like something between a paddle steamer and a jet boat. For a second I even thought I saw a rainbow above him.

While the low angle of the sunlight made the scene beautiful it also had its drawbacks. From time to time the deadly combination of direct sunlight and the very intense reflections off the water meant I could barely see which direction I should go. I was grateful for some protection afforded by the small visor fitted to the front of my helmet but its use was limited.

I ran aground on two separate occasions after missing not-so-subtle variations in the river, like a sharp right-hand turn. Half-blinded, I jumped out of my boat and floundered through the shallows toward deeper water. If I had been a fish I would have been a disgrace but fortunately I was a kayaker and in this race running aground seemed very popular. I was seldom alone in my distress.

I made some useful observations: the water gets very shallow when the waves caused by the kayak begin to break quietly beside you. The last thing I would hear before I ran aground was the unmistakable sound of a gently breaking wave and my rudder dragging on the stones. And I noticed that running aground is nearly always preceded by the muffled tonk, tonk, tonk sound of your rudder dragging on the river stones. When a number of kayakers are crossing the shallows together it sounds like a flock of underwater geese.

I learnt a few other lessons. A good sign that you have missed the correct place to turn is when the five kayakers just in front of you get out of their boats and stand up in ankle-deep water. This gave rise to another lesson: not everyone in front of you knows where he or she is going.

As I paddled on, the low hills immediately flanking the river seemed to be closing in up ahead. The river meandered over to the left of the valley and into the shade of a large dirt-faced cliff. I followed the procession of kayakers along the main flow as it swung around to the right and parallel to the cliff face.

I noticed the water was draining out of my braid and transferring to a new braid at the base of the cliff to my left. From above, the river must have looked like a giant ladder. It was as if I was paddling down the right-hand length of the ladder while at every opportunity the water escaped down the rungs to the left side. Each rung was in fact a narrow but steep chute of water.

The first few chutes looked fairly innocuous and I watched as kayakers in front of me peeled off one by one down the chute of their choice. At first I wondered where everyone was going but then noticed that up ahead my braid of the river narrowed to a trickle. Each chute had taken more and more water away and soon there would be nothing to paddle in. My braid was dying. I had to leave it and I had to do it soon.

I had left it too late to take the next chute but as I passed I looked down it in horror. It was alarmingly steeper than the previous one and at the bottom it met the full fury of what was now the main flow of the river. The point where they met was a twisting cauldron of kayak-chewing malevolence.

I quickly determined I had to take the next chute before they got any worse. I was almost alone now. Only two kayakers were left in my braid. One was an older man who powered past me in a long narrow boat, his face set with a grim look of intensity. The other was a very anxious-looking woman in a pink kayak. With a growing concern of my own I set a course for the next chute. The anxious woman had stopped paddling with any conviction and smiled weakly at me as I passed. She was clearly having grave doubts too.

Up ahead Mr Intensity seemed to have almost missed the next chute when at the last minute he violently swung his boat left and charged down it. The assuredness of his action gave me confidence as I neared the point where he had disappeared. I arrived at the top and looked down. It was wider and nowhere near as steep as the previous chute and I was greatly relieved. While I still had to contend with a sharp right-hand turn into rapids at the bottom I felt much more optimistic about my chances.

It was a shame then that I completely messed it up. I came down the chute way faster than I thought I would and instead of turning hard left at the bottom, paralysed with fear, I simply shot across the river and ploughed into the bank on the other side. I lurched forward at the impact and for the briefest moment I teetered on the brink of capsize. But somehow I didn't go over. Instead the back of the kayak was slowly pushed downstream by the force of the water and the nose ever so slowly turned until I was facing upstream – the complete opposite of the direction I wanted to go.

The next few minutes may have been the most humiliating of my short kayaking career. One by one a large number of kayakers filed past on their way downstream. While they were all busy contending with the rapids most had just enough time to snatch a surprised look at me followed by a smile or a smirk. One stunning wit in a distinctive blue kayak and sporting a cheeky grin had the brilliance to remind me I was going the wrong way. Talk about kicking a man when he's down. I resisted the temptation to take a wild swing at him with my paddle. To heighten my feelings of embarrassment I then had to watch the anxious woman in the pink kayak come down the same chute grimacing in fear, doing the last half with her eyes shut, and at the bottom executing a faultless turn downstream so that she was gone in an instant.

I sat forlornly facing upstream, waiting for a break in the line of kayaks coming down the river until I could attempt a U-turn. I felt very self-conscious and not unlike the driver of a car stalled in the middle of a busy intersection. Finally my gap came. I carefully poked the nose of the kayak out into the main flow. While I balanced precariously the water caught it quite suddenly and dragged it downstream. The kayak flicked around and I was pointing in the direction I should have gone long before now. Gathering what remaining shreds of dignity I could muster I sat up straight, collected myself and with a few strokes of the paddle I was finally on my way again.

I rejoined the long line of paddlers as they continued to make their way downstream. The main flow of water stayed over to the left-hand side of the valley and for the next while we were hard up against hills and in their shadows. While it was nice to have a break from paddling directly into the sunlight, I soon missed its warmth. In the shadows the water took on a deeper hue that made it look cold and uninviting.

Up ahead, at the point where I would be exiting the shadows of the hill, I saw a series of rapids. I peered into the distance, trying to make out what I was going to be up against. I could see the kayakers already in the rapids weaving this way and that while water splashed about in all directions. It looked challenging. At the same time I became aware of another kayaker beside me. He wore a blue helmet with what looked like a small plastic animal pinned to the top as if it had been crucified. He nodded toward the rapids, looked at me and smiled in an unconcerned manner. 'The Rock Garden,' he said.

I had heard about the Rock Garden only that morning. Standing with my group of 10 cyclists before the start I had overheard two cyclists discussing places to be wary of on the river. The Rock Garden stood out. It sounded scary. While those around listened in various states of anxiety the two men talked about how at the Rock Garden the river forcefully crashed its way through a collection of large, partially submerged boulders and how the difficult parts kept changing from year to year. Once their audience was captivated they began to amuse themselves by telling progressively more outrageous stories of huge rapids, dangerous rocks and the near-death experiences of friends and acquaintances.

And now this place of danger lay just ahead.

I was feeling apprehensive but decided my best bet was to follow the man in the blue helmet. I hoped his lack of concern was based on confidence.

I slowed my paddle stroke and let him ease ahead. I wanted him just far enough ahead so I could mimic his moves but avoid him if he turned out to be a kayaking fool.

As we entered the top of the Rock Garden the surrounding water began to chop up as it met the first of the unseen rocks. The slope of the river seemed to steepen and my speed increased alarmingly. I glanced ahead and immediately saw what I was up against. It was hideous. There was water splashing about in all directions and rocks everywhere. Some stuck out of the water while others barely broke the surface. Still others were completely underwater but causing mayhem on the surface. Whatever, they all contributed to the same effect. They impeded the smooth flow of the water and anyone that sought to flow with it. I was being forced left one second and right the next. Trying to control the kayak was a nightmare.

Up ahead, a big rock just below the surface produced a hump of water in front of it. It looked harmless enough until I paddled past and saw that it concealed a huge, gaping hole immediately behind it, a crevice of the river. The next one was worse. Barely in control I couldn't avoid paddling over another hump and gasped in shock and surprise as the nose of my kayak dropped into the huge hole behind and ploughed deep into the wall of water on the other side. The wall was so steep it was breaking and falling down on itself into the hole. My forward momentum drove the nose of the kayak into the wall and deeper and deeper under the water. Time seemed to stand still as the nose of the boat hovered underwater as if lost in indecision. For the briefest moment my courage almost failed. But slowly, almost imperceptibly at first, the laws of physics began to prevail and the air trapped in the nose of the boat began to force it back toward the surface, shedding buckets of water as it did so. I was free, but only for a moment: there was more to come.

Up ahead I noticed a nasty boulder protruding a few inches out of the water and started to steer away from it. I pushed hard on my left rudder pedal but it didn't seem to respond much. The nose of the kayak began to drift slightly left while the flow of the water continued to carry me directly toward the rock. I began to paddle furiously in an attempt to avoid a collision but it was too late. Or so I thought. At the last second I cringed and waited for impact, but it never came. As I passed by the rock

I saw why. In front of it the water that had welled up into a big bulge pushed me away at the last second. I had discovered quite by accident an important lesson: that even a near-miss was good enough to avoid most obstacles.

A few seconds later I learnt another lesson. As I looked up ahead for the next obstacle a flurry of activity caught my eye. I watched as a kayaker made his way around a fair-sized rock with an interesting technique. As he approached the rock he began to paddle forward more vigorously before making an abrupt turn to one side. His kayak veered left and after passing the rock he swung the nose back right and straightened out. All at once I understood what I had done wrong and what I needed to do. To bring the rudder into play I needed to paddle harder. If I just sat in the boat and floated downstream with the water, the rudder couldn't work. Like on a ship with no power a rudder is useless. It needed water flowing past it, and for that to happen I had to paddle. The faster I paddled the more effective the rudder would become and the less likely I would be at the whim of the currents. It was a revelation. I charged down the last section of the Rock Garden with renewed confidence. The only obstacle that presented itself was a smallish, partially submerged rock. I charged at it while pushing hard on the left rudder pedal. I lurched left. When I was far enough out to the left I swung hard right and easily avoided the rock. I shot down the last rapids and all at once I was out.

I rested amongst the chaos in the long deep pool at the bottom of the rapid. There were kayakers everywhere. Only half of them were in their boats. Some were trying to swim, paddle in hand, after their boats; one man had his boat but no paddle, while others floated toward the bank with nothing. Kayakers who had negotiated the rapid with boat and paddle intact drifted slowly downstream fiddling with this and that and generally collecting themselves after what was probably the most frightening experience of their short kayaking careers. On the stony river bank there were three kayaks being emptied and a woman sitting alone. She had a blanket around her shoulders and her face in her hands. It didn't look like she intended to continue.

As the river safety team whipped around the pool reuniting people with their equipment I moved on. I was greatly relieved to have got this far but in the back of my mind I knew this was just the prelude. The main event was still off in the distance, out of sight but there just the same. It was where I would pass or fail; it was where I would live or die and thoughts of it stalked my conscious mind like an unfamiliar shadow in a darkened room. The gorge was coming.

Chapter 18

Water Worries

The Waimakariri Gorge, although tiny in comparison, is New Zealand's answer to the Grand Canyon. Here the foothills flanking the river plain gradually grow in height and finally close in, collecting all the braids together and narrowing the wide expanse of the river down to a single flow of water. Over thousands of years the water has chiselled out of the solid rock a narrow path some 25 kilometres long through the mountains. In many places its dark walls tower ominously over the river like huge stone sentinels. It is a spectacular place, and an environment to be treated with respect. Once you have entered the gorge, you have few options but to continue on to its end.

Most of my kayaking fears revolved around stories I had heard about the gorge section of the river. I had heard tales of huge rapids, massive pressure waves and whirlpools big enough to swallow a jet boat. I had heard of broken kayaks, broken paddles and broken people. I had heard stories of great drama: of friends swept away only to be found hours later clinging to rock faces way downstream, shivering with cold and barely alive; of kayakers falling out of their kayaks and not being able to find a beach to land on for hundreds of metres; of groups rescued by helicopter and of cold nights spent huddled together for warmth beside broken boats and rising floodwaters. Don told me that once, in a strong wind, he had seen a man blown across the river in his kayak like a skipping stone unleashed by an unseen hand.

With all this in mind it was no wonder I was feeling nervous. But I knew I wouldn't be alone with my concerns. Over the last couple of days I had overheard many people talking nervously about the kayak section – like me, most were novices concerned about the gorge. Together we listened to the stories with dry mouths and in reverent silence. At night we'd lie awake with recurring visions of great churning masses of evil black water mercilessly tossing terrified kayakers about like corks between jagged walls of razor-sharp rock.

Thankfully there are times when the reality is a little different, and the gorge is quite tame. The difference between a pleasant jaunt down the river and a spectacular death pretty much depends on the amount of water flowing through, which can vary from a low flow of around 40 cubic metres per second (or cumecs, as this is generally abbreviated to) to hideously unspeakable amounts. At around 40 cumecs the water is generally channelled into just one narrow flow. The kayaker is forced to follow that flow wherever it may lead. This means that if the whole flow of water ploughs straight into a rock face the kayaker must go there too.

Where the water meets the rock face the surface gurgles and bubbles about angrily as unseen pressures below tear it this way and that before it falls away downstream. Some of the water is forced on the upstream side of the main flow and temporarily thwarted from its downstream journey. It swirls around and around in angry whirlpools on the surface while underneath it clutches and claws at the oncoming flow trying to cross it and continue its journey downstream.

The experts say that the trick in this situation is to stay with the main flow of water, but on the downstream side of where the torrent hits the rock, even if it means going uncomfortably close to the rock face itself, while pointing the nose of your boat downstream and somehow staying relaxed. Of course this seems like insanity to the novice kayaker – akin to paddling up to the jaws of death just to count the teeth. But at 40 cumecs you might not have a choice. The nastiest route might be the only option.

Presumably, the advantage of kayaking in 40 cumecs is that the river is more tame than when the water is higher. But that does not always hold true: at 80 cumecs the same rapid may barely exist, with the deeper water reducing the effect the rocks have on the surface to little more than a few ripples. At 80 cumecs the river is wider and the water level a little higher. This means there are more opportunities to cut corners and avoid difficult spots – a method of kayaking often described as taking the 'chicken route', although despite the name there is no shame in doing so. Eighty cumecs is a lot of water to be ploughing into rock faces so following the main flow can be a far nastier proposition than it is at 40 cumecs. At 80 cumecs and above the 'chicken route' might more aptly be named the 'sanity route'.

At 200 cumecs the gorge can become a seething, twisting cauldron of kayak-swallowing evil, and taking the 'chicken route' shortcuts may involve crossing swirling whirlpools that grab at a kayak and quite suddenly jerk it in another direction, throwing the shocked kayaker off balance and into the frigid water. However, at 200 cumecs taking a wildly swirling chicken route might be a better option than paddling with the main flow. As it smashes into a rock face it sends great torrents of water belching up before collapsing heavily down on itself in a wild, angry froth, and at 200 cumecs the nice little rapid that seemed so tame at 80 cumecs may have turned into a series of big standing waves. These waves rear up and fall away in much the same way as ordinary rapids do but on a much grander scale. A short kayak goes up and down them like a small yacht in an ocean of big waves. A long kayak might ride from one crest to another like a super tanker in a storm.

At 200 cumecs a good kayaker might be able to paddle just off to either side of the standing waves and experience a safe and lightning-quick ride to the bottom of the rapid. But the margin for error is small. Usually a few feet either side of the safe paddling zone is an eddy, which is essentially a backflow of water heading upstream. The faster the water is coming down the rapid then the faster the eddy is going back up its sides. If the nose of your kayak happens to stray across the eddy line, as it is called, the best you can hope for a few seconds later is to still be in your boat facing upstream. There are dangers here for all types of racing kayaks: the shorter kayak might nose-dive into a wave and stall just long enough to tip over; a longer kayak might bend or break in the middle if it is stretched across two waves. Given the right conditions anything is possible in the gorge.

With all these thoughts swirling around my head I was starting to feel a little nervous. I pushed them away. I didn't want to get too far ahead of myself. I still had plenty of braided river to deal with before I even got to the gorge and I was going to need my full concentration to get through that first.

* * *

As the hills pulled away from the river I entered a huge gravel plain. The river split and split again, each braid having less and less water. I followed a couple of other kayakers into a braid that looked as if it had slightly more water than some of the earlier choices. We raced down the narrow channel, sometimes very close to one or other bank. All around I could see the paddles of other kayakers in different braids bobbing up and down through the heat haze and the prickly gorse bushes that dotted the plain. Clearly there were a range of different opinions as to which of the many braids were worth pursuing. I had no idea how far my one would go but assumed that sooner or later all the water would end up in the same place. I hoped the braid I had chosen didn't turn to a trickle before it got there.

A few hundred metres away I saw a forlorn bunch of kayakers walking with boats up on one shoulder in search of deeper water. I felt sorry for them. There was no guarantee the next braid they got into was going to be any better. Another group of kayakers was struggling in a braid parallel to ours. They had almost run out of water but were making enough progress to encourage them to stay in their boats as they struggled on. One paddled wildly, thrashing at the water, trying and trying to keep forward momentum through brute force. With each stroke the horrible clanking sound of his expensive Kevlar paddle being clawed across the shallow-water stones made me cringe. He was spending an awful lot of energy in a sort of frantic panic, but admittedly he was making better progress than the others behind him. They were trying a combination of two methods: while paddling strongly, albeit with a lot less conviction than the chap in front of them, two of them had added the technique of wriggling about and hopping in their boats. I figured the technique was intended to allow more water under the kayak and thereby keep it moving. This looked delightfully like a Monty Python skit: I envisaged kayakers trying to bounce their boats down a cobbled London street. The last of the group had given up paddling altogether and was trying to push himself along with his hands while the paddle sat redundant on the spray skirt. I imagined his cold hands trying to grip the paddle when he finally could use it again.

I paddled on and caught up to the two men I had followed into the braid in the first place and the three of us seemed to be powering along. I found that draughting closely behind the kayak directly in front made paddling easier, although time after time I nearly rode up on to the chap's rudder. I'm not exactly sure of the hydrodynamics involved but I guess it has something to do with the lead kayak disturbing the water enough to allow the second kayak to glide through in the wake. Perhaps it was like draughting behind another cyclist or perhaps there is another reason. To be honest, I didn't give a toss. It was a hell of a lot easier paddling right behind him so I did it. I didn't need to understand it any more than I need to understand electricity to turn on a light.

As we charged down our narrow but powerful little braid I noticed that the further we went the more it began to fill with water and the faster it got. Another small braid joined ours and then another, increasing our pace even more. It was exciting speeding along in such close confines.

The speed did, however, have its downside. Every now and then the braid turned sharp corners and once we encountered a difficult S-bend. These corners scared the hell out of me. I'd be barrelling along and then quite suddenly be confronted with a 90-degree turn. Six-metre-long kayaks are a bit like buses in that they don't turn 90 degrees very well without a lot of room. I'd end up getting halfway around to find the kayak's nose barely missing the rocks lining the river bank. One hit could see me tipped over in an instant. The prospect of being dragged along upside down in two feet of water with my head tapping a steady rhythm on the rocks below wasn't appealing.

The two blokes in front of me were having similar problems, except in addition they periodically had me ramming into them from behind. They tried a variety of turning methods but were largely unsuccessful and their boats took a battering.

It soon got worse. The three of us came flying around one small bend to find the next bend was overhung by a series of gorse bushes. A number of branches from each bush hung out into the main flow as it pushed hard up against the left-hand bank. Any kayaker that didn't take immediate evasive action was destined to be taken right into the gorse.

'Oh shit,' yelled the first bloke as he realised what was about to happen. He paddled wildly to get the nose of his boat over to the right and away from the gorse but the flow of water drove him mercilessly toward it. It was too late. Catching him with his head up and exposed, the branches dragged across his face and swished about his neck. His head was forced right back as if he was doing the limbo. Immediately the balance of the kayak was affected and he began to wobble violently from side to side. Just when I thought he was going to fall out he got an opportunity to change his position. In the small gap before the next gorse bush he thrust his head violently forward so that his nose almost touched the front deck of his kayak. It was a lucky break. The remaining bushes proceeded to harmlessly drag over the back of his helmet.

He came out the other side and let loose with the most complete set of obscenities I have ever heard. He then yelled a few of the better-known ones again for good measure before paddling off wildly.

In the few seconds we had the other kayaker and I did all we could to position our approach to avoid the bulk of the gorse and choose the path of least resistance. At the last moment we both ducked forward and slipped through the bushes with little more than a few scratches.

A strange bond sometimes develops between people in times of crisis or shared experience, and for us that time was now. As the braid widened I pulled up beside him and we were both all smiles as we started chatting about our good fortune to choose the right braid, the speed of the water, the nice weather and how cool it was to not get all scratched to hell. It struck me that this was a friendship based on smugly witnessing someone else's pain and the joy of avoiding it oneself, but what can you do? Human nature can be like that and it pays not to examine such things too closely.

Not too far ahead, and I'm guessing pretty much oblivious to everything except about a thousand scratches, our fellow kayaker continued to charge into the distance.

The braid we were in snaked its way over to the low hills on the right-hand side of the plain. We made an easy left-hand turn as our braid morphed into the wide and shallow fast-moving water at the base of the hills. We were now near the bottom of the gravel-covered plain and all the various braids that had crossed it were coming together again. More and more water poured in as it found the main flow. Other kayakers began to regularly pop out in front of us as they too found the main flow. Looks of utter relief suggested annoying groundings and arduous walks in search of deeper water, while other more competitive kayakers wore frustrated, agitated glares that told of lost time, lost speed and lost places.

Further on we saw a large group of kayakers shoot in one by one from what looked like a narrow, fast-moving side stream. They wobbled about as they regained control and paddled off. I knew from bitter experience that it was no easy task joining a flow of fast water as it thundered at you from side on and I watched the different approaches with interest. The first three kayakers were poetry in motion and made it look very simple. They slowed their stroke before leaning delicately downstream and briefly hovering over the paddle. As they did this the bottom of the kayak was briefly exposed to the approaching flow of water, which caressed the boat upright and in the same motion gracefully swept it around the turn and away. It was beautiful to watch.

Another fellow, however, shot out into the main flow and almost crossed to the other bank before making a shaky left-hand turn and carrying on downstream, while another wobbled into the main flow leaning toward the new current instead of away, so that the water caught the side of his kayak and flipped it over. He soon appeared from underneath it, flailing about with his paddle and yelping about the cold. He was almost run down by the next kayaker, who nearly tipped over also, trying to avoid him. The chap in the water soon reacquainted himself with his boat and was trying to swim it to shore when I passed. I noticed his kayak was almost completely submerged and full of water. This was a bad sign. I assumed his buoyancy bags must have deflated. It was not going to be easy to get it to the river bank: a kayak full of water weighs a massive amount and becomes almost impossible to move anywhere it doesn't feel like going. I didn't envy him the difficult task of trying to stop the boat, let alone empty it once he finally got into water shallow enough to stand up and attempt it.

But I had problems of my own. My nerves were returning. As we crossed smaller and smaller gravel plains I knew we were getting closer. I couldn't see the gorge but I could feel its presence in every little mistake I made. An overcorrected wobble here, a jittery paddle stroke there. Each time the hills closed in on both sides and I thought we were almost there, the winding river would reveal another small plain to cross. Finally I looked ahead and saw the hills on both sides had come down to a point in the shadows a few hundred metres away. There was nowhere else for the river to go. It flowed directly toward a large, ominous rock face and slithered past it into the gloom. I was there.

Chapter 19

The Gorge

The river swept up to a large, dark rock face before spilling around to the right and out of sight behind another steep hill. I could feel the anxiety building with every paddle stroke but I paddled on. Another kayaker slowly pulled up beside me and soon passed by, grinning happily. Perhaps the gorge wouldn't be so bad. After all, the flow was running at around 70 cumecs so it shouldn't be too difficult. I looked around and was comforted by the fact that there were now kayakers everywhere. At least I would have plenty of company.

As I got closer to the rock face that marked the entrance to the gorge, my eyes were drawn down to a movement at its base. Where the rock met the water I saw an odd sight. Caught in a patch of still water hard up against the face were two kayakers. The one closest to the rock was facing downstream but was trapped on the inside of another kayaker who was facing upstream. I stared at them. How on earth had they got into this predicament? The chap on the inside seemed very anxious to get going but he couldn't get the nose of his boat out past a section of rock or the other kayak. As I got closer I saw that he was protesting loudly about being boxed in and at the same time was trying to push the nose of the other kayaker's boat back out into the flow. This was clearly upsetting the poor chap facing upstream, whose own shouts of protest increased in volume the more his boat wobbled about. Paddles started flailing about as they both tried to keep upright. As I passed them it looked as if they were about to come to blows.

I had gone another 20 metres when I heard a shout of alarm and I half-turned just in time to see a third kayaker totally misjudge the turn at the rock face and awkwardly barrel into the chap facing upstream. The impact saw both of them disappear under water as they capsized, then reappear with a lot of shouting and gesticulating.

Now that I was in the gorge proper I nervously wondered what to expect. As I paddled through a relatively wide calm section I noticed ahead the water began to flow over to the right. As I got closer I saw that the slope of the river had steepened and the water had gathered considerable momentum. The next section looked difficult. Just around the corner I could make out some large rocks jutting out of the middle of the river while the right-hand bank was lined with its own array of jagged rocks. I watched as a kayaker just ahead stayed near the fast water in the middle as he negotiated the corner but then proceeded to move well over to the left-hand side. I tried to follow his every move. I got a little scare when it took longer than expected to avoid one of the big rocks that dominated the middle of the river. It seemed so far away when I started to paddle left to avoid it but then suddenly I was almost upon it. A few quick paddle strokes and a solid push on the left rudder and I swept just past its left side. The buffer wave bouncing off the rock's flank pushed me further to safety.

I exited the corner and my unofficial guide immediately paddled hard for the right-hand side of the river. I looked beyond him to see that if I continued my present path the water on the left side would soon lead me into a nasty little bluff with spray-moistened black walls glistening like wet steel. I paddled strongly forward while working my rudder and got as far away as possible towards the right side of the river.

Despite my fear I was learning. I could see that while I needed to concentrate on the water around my boat I also needed to look well ahead and be aware of where I wanted to be long before I got there. While I had been doing that to some extent on the plains, it was more critical in the gorge where the water moved much faster.

Over the next 10 minutes I negotiated my way through a series of tricky spots. It was exciting. With water hitting bluffs head-on and churning wildly, I rode the calmer lines between the brawling eddies. I began to feel confident. I got used to the idea of looking forward to the next piece of water as soon as I had cleared the last. I was becoming accustomed to the sights and sounds of the gorge.

Suddenly I heard a sound I didn't recognise. My senses sharpened and I strained to hear. It was a barely audible thumping sound emanating from somewhere further down the river. I immediately feared the worst and wondered if I wasn't hearing the thunder of some huge rapid lying in wait for unsuspecting novices like myself. But I was wrong. Two minutes later a helicopter roared over my head and thundered off down the gorge swaying out gracefully on each turn. I caught a glimpse of Judkins grinning maniacally as he hurtled past in his glass fishbowl.

In the real world I was making good progress down the gorge. My guide had been a great help but had gradually pulled away. Although I could still see him I wasn't close enough to see exactly which line he took through the tricky spots so I looked around for further guidance. I knew exactly what I was looking for. I wanted to follow a competent but cautious kayaker who wasn't going too fast for me.

There were plenty of other kayakers just up ahead and I determined to try and catch them. It was harder than I expected. On the long straight sections of river that we soon moved into it seemed that no matter how hard I paddled I hardly made any impression on the distance between us. But luck was on my side. A kayaker ahead of the group I was chasing suddenly tipped out of his kayak, turning sideways and temporarily blocking the group. Soon I had halved the distance between us.

As I got closer I found I was definitely getting more familiar with the patterns of the gorge and for the next 15 minutes I did, by my standards, pretty well. I paddled from this side to that, avoiding the worst of the difficult bits by cutting corners, taking everything that even vaguely looked like a chicken route and all the while gaining on the kayakers ahead of me.

As I caught up to the group ahead I started to look for someone to follow. I soon worked out that there were two types of kayaker to avoid: the novice and the expert. The novice kayakers were fairly obvious. Like me most were learning as they went. Those that spun round the wrong way and crashed into rock faces, and each other, eliminated themselves and were soon left far behind. While following fellow novices was dangerous, so too was tailing the other end of the spectrum – the expert. The expert was more difficult to spot. He or she might take the easy line through a number of tricky sections without doing anything fancy to show their skill, and then unexpectedly extricate themselves from what appeared to be an impossible spot. I was happily following an expert just like this and when relatively close behind him and following his seemingly educated lead, suddenly found myself in a pickle. With no time to back out I realised I was being led down a hideous path straight at a huge mound of water bulging up from the depths in front of an ugly black rock face before it twisted violently into a hole. The expert rode up onto the bulge as cool as a cucumber and as he was swept toward the hole he avoided it with two powerful paddle strokes and a flick of the hip that would have made a matador proud. In an instant he had passed the danger and was gone.

I, however, was left with two insane choices. Either I could attempt to mimic the amazing contortion I had just witnessed or I could shut my eyes. I shut my eyes. A few seconds later I opened them to find I had survived and was still upright in my kayak. I was ecstatic. Now this was a technique I could use. Stuff all those fancy kayaking strokes – all I had to do was to go in at the correct angle and hope for the best. Way to go! Boy was I on top of my game or what? I would revolutionise kayaking technique with this one for sure. A few minutes later when the adrenalin had worn off I calmed down. Shutting my eyes was stupid and I knew it. I decided not to do it again. It just wasn't safe.

The safety of competitors has always been Robin Judkins' highest priority. In over 20 years of the Coast to Coast there have been no deaths. With so many competitors travelling through an area of such rugged terrain this is an impressive statistic. It has on occasions, however, been close. On the morning of the start of the two-day race in 1999 two competitors were riding their bikes in the pre-dawn dark from the Kumara racecourse, where they had camped the night, to the bike stands near Kumara beach. Without warning they were hit from behind by a car on its way to the start area. Both cyclists were badly injured. One suffered a brain injury and was unconscious for a week. Neither cyclist had rear lights on their bike. On another occasion in 1985 a kayaker almost did drown but was resuscitated. It turned out he had tied the paddle to his wrist and couldn't free himself from it when he got into difficulty. Not a good idea.

If you run an event like the Coast to Coast for long enough, eventually you will see it all. But it's what you do with that knowledge that counts. To Robin Judkins every mistake a competitor made was an opportunity.

He learnt from their mistakes and if he could do something about it he did. If necessary he modified the rules of his race. After noticing a number of big bunch crashes in the two-day event he banned aero bars. The number of crashes dramatically reduced.

Heavy rain in some of the early years of the event taught Judkins the need for adequate survival gear. He insisted competitors carry first aid kits, extra clothing and food in the mountains and he introduced checks to make sure the competitors did so. Those that didn't have the right gear were stopped and sent back to get it. In the 2004 event that gear probably saved lives. Heavy rain filled the rivers and only the first 50 or so made it through the run section. Wet and very cold most of the others were rescued by helicopter. Some waited hours for rescue. The survival gear they carried at Judkins' insistence was all that saved them from hypothermia or worse.

The most likely place to have real problems with safety in a race like the Coast to Coast is the river section. Ensuring the safety of hundreds of kayakers on a river like the Waimakariri is no mean feat, and while Judkins has insisted from the very early days of the event that competitors must be adequately prepared for the river he has always had extra support available. I had noticed the short-boat kayakers stationed at various rapids above the gorge, and in the gorge itself I also knew Judkins relied on jet boats.

The jet boats are a kind of double-edged sword to the novice kayaker. On the one hand they are a source of great comfort. They sit just downstream of the biggest, most difficult rapids and the nastiest bluffed corners, their crews poised at the ready to whip out and rescue anyone who needs assistance. They patrol the river and at the end of the day they take out those who for whatever reason can't continue. If you get into trouble they are a godsend.

Not all the jet boats on the river, however, are there as support for the race. Some are transporting fisherman or sightseers or joyriders blasting around and having a fun day out. They are like the semi-trucks of the liquid highway. You'll be quietly kayaking along while listening to the harmless gurgling of the river when all of a sudden a deafening blast of noise explodes around the corner behind you. Kayakers scatter. The noise gets closer and closer and when you are sure you will be run down and killed they blow by on the other side of the river. The occupants wave happily in your direction, oblivious to the fact they scared the hell out of you. You make a rude gesture back at them but they think you are returning their greeting and so they smile and wave again. Then they are gone. It's about then that the boat wash hits you. These waves sneak up behind and rock you wildly from side to side just as you begin to relax, leaving your nerves shattered.

Having settled on my resolve to keep safety first, I progressed further through the gorge. I was finding it a difficult place in which to concentrate for long periods of time. Crossing the plains before the gorge I had needed to be alert constantly as I chose my route, assessed various braids, and negotiated rapids. The gorge was different. I would come out of a tricky spot, having survived a certain dunking, wide-eyed and pumped up with adrenalin and ready to take on the world, only to find that the next 10 minutes was like paddling across a millpond. In the absence of any gut-wrenching challenges I would gradually relax as I took in the scenery so that the next nasty corner would sneak up out of the blue and I would suddenly be scrambling to get into position.

I was happily paddling along one of these stretches of slow-moving water when up from behind came another odd sound. I listened intently. It sounded a lot like a squeak. What's more it was rhythmic. It was almost like someone was coming up behind me on a squeaky bicycle. I looked behind as best I could but there was nothing to see but a few other kayakers quietly paddling away in their own little dream worlds. The sound got closer and closer until a chap pulled up beside me. He was about to pass me when I realised the noise was coming from his paddle.

'Gidday,' he said quietly as he noticed my stare.

'Hi there,' I responded. 'Where is that sound coming from?'

He half-smiled in a wry sort of way that told me he had fielded this question a few times before. 'It's from the paddle,' he said. 'After about an hour's paddling it starts up and doesn't stop until I do.'

'Oh.' I said, leaving it that. I didn't want to embarrass him. A long silence ensued. He stopped trying to pass me and settled into an easy rhythm as he squeaked away beside me. It was quite mesmerising. We paddled along together side by side, in perfect time, without looking at each other. For a number of minutes the only sounds were the quiet splash of parted water and the metronomic squeak, squeak, squeak of his paddle.

After what seemed a long time he spoke again. 'It's something to do with my right hand. I've tried different paddles but nothing stops it.' He obviously wanted to talk about it.

'Have you tried gloves?'

'Yes, but I find them difficult to paddle with.'

'Oh.'

'I've tried different things on my hand, too, but they make the paddle too slippery.'

'Yes, I know what you mean,' I replied, remembering my own experience with the sunblock.

There was another long silence. Well, when I say silence, I mean silence punctuated with the constant squeak of his paddle.

It was relentless. Squeak, squeak, squeak.

I started playing games with it, counting as many squeaks as I could before he made a change in speed or tempo. On one straight stretch he did 45 perfectly-spaced strokes with his right paddle before he threw in a few quick ones to avoid a rock.

Next I started thinking of songs that fit the beat. Frank Sinatra was perfect. 'Fly me to the (squeak) and let me (squeak) among the stars ...'

After a while the squeak got to me and I wanted to laugh out loud. I had just recovered my composure when without warning the squeak changed up an octave. I could barely contain myself. I took a quick look at him and gave a slight grin as he noticed my glance. He looked embarrassed. Like a dog with one of those neck collars on to stop them from scratching a stitched wound.

He was like the leper of the kayak section. I felt terrible. I didn't want to make anyone feel like that but at the same time I felt the laughter coming up from the depths of my being. I suppressed it, just.

All the while the squeaking continued.

When I'd had about all I could take I slowed my paddling down a bit. He matched it, so I stopped altogether and began to play with the buckles on my lifejacket. He seemed unsure what to do and hung round like a stray dog for a while before he eventually squeaked off into the distance.

About this time I was beginning to hear the call of nature. It had been getting louder and louder for the last few hours but now it was beginning to scream.

I examined my options. I could stop and get out of the boat but I really didn't want to. Stopping just didn't seem right. It was a race, after all. I imagined myself standing on the riverbank, cheerily waving to the next 50 kayakers with a goofy grin on my face as I stood there spraying the rocks. Yeah right. I decided I was going to have to pee in my boat.

I kept paddling and tried to start but nothing happened. It wasn't like I didn't need to, in fact it was the complete opposite. I was desperate to. It suddenly struck me why they call it relieving oneself. I needed relief and I needed it badly. I started what I hoped would be a pre-urination routine by trying to relax. After about a minute I realised I was wasting my time. I couldn't possibly keep paddling and try to relax. So I stopped paddling. The kayak glided forward for a while before coming almost to a stop. I sat there and waited. Nothing happened.

A bloke paddled past and looked at me suspiciously. It didn't seem right to explain to a complete stranger that I was simply trying to pee so I said nothing. He continued to look at me suspiciously. I didn't quite know what else to do so I smiled weakly. I immediately felt stupid. He regarded me even more suspiciously. Oh great, I thought; now he thinks I'm gay. If I had been playing with the buckles on my lifejacket he probably wouldn't have given me a second glance, but because I was sitting virtually motionless I looked as if I was up to no good. He sneered at me and paddled off.

Another kayaker soon passed and so I started to play with the buckles on my lifejacket. Still nothing happened. A woman paddled past. It was the last straw. Frustrated, I gave up and started paddling again.

I couldn't believe it. Back home I had the bladder of a 70-year-old man but today for some reason I was the Hoover Dam. I paddled on slowly, trying to think of rushing water and the joys of urinating but it was no use so I did the only thing I could think of: I drank some more water. Within a minute it had started.

While it might have taken a bit to get going there was no stopping it now. In no time it became an uncontrollable torrent and now I was peeing for all I was worth. I peed and I peed and I peed. When I thought

I had finished I peed some more. When I was absolutely and completely sure I had finally finished and there was no way I could possibly pass another drop it all started up again and I peed for another 20 seconds.

Finally it stopped. Now I don't mean to overstate the relief or glorify something as mundane as having a pee but without a shadow of a doubt this pee was the greatest I have ever had. In terms of relief it ranked as number one, just ahead of the time I was seven and didn't want to leave a Batman movie to go to the toilet. After weeks of waiting there was no way in hell I was leaving the greatest movie in the history of mankind just to go to the toilet.

My four-year-old daughter lives by similar logic. She is quite happy to wet herself and suffer all the associated discomfort just to continue a game with her dolls. Despite the obvious drawbacks it does show a commendable commitment to play. As the warm pool of urine sloshed around my own feet I understood.

After another long calm stretch of water I made a difficult left-hand turn in a violently swirling piece of water at the base of a bluff. As I recovered my composure and prepared to paddle off I thought I could hear a distant rumbling. I strained to get a better grasp on what the sound was. It wasn't loud enough to be either a helicopter or a jet boat and although the sound was faint it didn't seem that far away. I was puzzled.

The answer came suddenly when I noticed a couple of kayakers not far ahead of me begin down a slope and then suddenly drop out of sight.

'Oh hell.' I knew what it was. A rapid. I had little time to prepare.

At the top of the slope I looked down and it was as if I was on the edge of a large amphitheatre. Water spilled into the amphitheatre from all sides, charging down the slope and meeting to form the top of the rapid.

It ran about 80 metres in length and sported a series of big waves that stood high as the water was thrown up by large rocks well below the surface. Beyond was the now-familiar post-rapid chaos. There was a jet boat working each side of the river while two or three kayakers floundered about in the water and a couple of others were getting back into their boats at the stony river banks.

As I started my descent I looked at where the rapid started and decided if at all possible I wanted to go down the left-hand edge, which looked the safest option as the right had large rocks jutting out of the water halfway down. I would have my work cut out for me: I was in the perfect spot to set up for a trip down the right side, but to get to the left I would have to paddle across to the far side while the water dragged me toward the middle. When I reached the start of the rapid I didn't want to be in the middle. If I did I would have to take on the huge waves.

I paddled like a maniac. For a second or two I wasn't sure I was going to make it. The water was splashing up in my face obscuring, my vision and the speed of the water sweeping me toward the top of the rapid caught me by surprise. I knew it was going to be close. The water parted for a second and I saw I was almost there. I put in three of the hardest strokes I could manage, turned slightly right to line up and hit the top section of the rapid almost exactly where I wanted to be. It was the perfect spot but I wasn't out of it yet.

I paddled just past the left-hand edge of the first big wave. It was huge. Don had told me it was important to keep paddling in rapids but I did the next best thing by slapping the water on each side at twice the rate I would have paddled. It worked well. Not only did it help me keep my balance but I kept my position just left of the waves. I sped down the line of waves with my heart pounding, my paddle flailing and water splashing everywhere. It was incredibly exciting. I could feel the eyes of the jet boat crews as I charged the last few metres and suddenly I had made it.

I was pumped. I let out a huge 'yahoo'. The jet boat boys grinned and I 'yahooed' again.

I looked around at the other kayakers who were still in various stages of boat retrieval and felt satisfied. I just couldn't believe I had come so far without falling out. Gee this is going well, I thought, as I carried on happily.

Paddling down a long straight, I was stunned to see the massive arch of a giant reddish-tinged rail bridge towering majestically over a bend in the river. It was a magnificent sight. The bridge straddled the gap between two very steep walls of a rugged ravine. I realised it must be one of the bridges crossed by the Transalpine Express on its traverse across the South Island between Christchurch and Greymouth. The route shadows the gorge and passes through the beautiful Southern Alps and is commonly regarded as one of the top ten scenic rail journeys in the world.

Deeply committed in the Gorge. Sometimes it all feels a bit overwhelming. Paul's Camera Shop

The Waimakariri Gorge: ominous rock walls, cold treacherous water. You know you've done well when you get to the bottom of a hair-raising rapid and there's a jet boat waiting to pick up competitors who've come to grief. Paul's Camera Shop

I had now been kayaking for three hours and I had had enough. As I suffered away, far below the bridge, I longed to be a passenger on anything that would get me out of this situation. My arms were tired, my bottom was numb and my legs were stiff. I couldn't get comfortable. I wanted to get out. I was sick of sitting cramped up in this rigid little Kevlar cockpit.

The finish couldn't come soon enough, but I had heard it would take about 50 minutes to an hour to reach the finish from some place called Woodstock. Woodstock marked the end of the gorge but there was absolutely no sign of the place.

I fantasised about pulling over to the bank, getting out and watching all the other kayakers go past while I sat in a large soft armchair with a nice cup of tea. But I knew I couldn't stop. I wouldn't. I would never allow myself to give in and admit defeat. For the second time in two days I had reached a real low point and was struggling to lift myself out.

I paddled on. There were fewer people around now. The weaker kayakers were somewhere behind me and the stronger ones were ahead.

Nothing much seemed to change. Even the river seemed monotonous. It flowed on and on relentlessly, each section looking much the same as the one before. There were no exciting rapids, no fast sections and no treacherously twisting bluffed corners to deal with. I became blasé.

Paddling down a small chute I momentarily lost balance, tipping to the right. I didn't tip far but it was far enough. I reacted slowly with my paddle. A simple slap at the water on the right side would have corrected the lean and bounced me back upright. By the time the two or three litres of urine and water had sloshed over to the right side of the boat I knew I wasn't coming back upright. I hit the water and the cold pierced me like a spear.

It was surreal. Here I was, upside down in my kayak. There was no sound and in the milky depths I could only just see my white knuckles still gripping the paddle just in front of my face.

I woke up. 'Crikey, I'm getting out of here.'

I let go the paddle, grabbed the spray skirt toggle and ripped it off the kayak. As water flooded the cockpit I twisted out of it and kicked myself free. I broke the surface and gratefully sucked in an overdue breath.

I grabbed the paddle and kayak and began swimming for the bank, making slow progress with only a leg-kick for propulsion until halfway there my foot touched the bottom. In no time I was in the shallows and wrestling water out of the boat. I strained to lift one of the ends off the ground but as the water flooded out the boat quickly became lighter. As soon as I could I flipped it over and got back in. It wasn't easy. Not only was I stiff from my long confinement but now I was cold as well.

It wasn't long before I was back into the grind of the marathon kayaker. Time passed slowly. Again it seemed that for long periods very little changed. From time to time someone would inch past and slowly creep off into the distance. I envied them. Not only were they still passing people but they would also finish sooner than me.

The finish. Oh, how I longed to be at the finish. To get out of my kayak and walk around, stretch my legs and... I suddenly remembered that I still had to bike 70 kilometres to the finish. It was almost overwhelming and as I paddled on I wondered how on earth I would have the energy to bike so far.

I began to notice I was hungry. I hadn't really eaten much since the start. I had snatched at some nuts but their oil made the paddle slippery in my hands and I'd had to go through the hand-wiping routine all over again. I had also grappled with a food bar with reasonable success. I had eaten half of it but when I'd gone back for the second half about 40 minutes later it was all soggy like a piece of bread in a bowl of soup.

It's not easy to eat in a kayak because when you are eating you are not paddling and if you are not paddling, while you might still be moving you are probably not going anywhere near where you want to.

I was hungry all right. To make matters worse when I came around the next bend I was greeted with the most divine smell imaginable. A few seconds later I saw two jet boats parked up at the side of the river and nearby a couple of families looked to be having a barbecue.

I was thinking what a great idea it was and how much I would love to be joining them when out of the corner of my eye I caught another movement. I almost stopped paddling. It was a figure I recognised immediately. Mr Colossus appeared out of the undergrowth, where I suspected he had been relieving himself, and with a cheery grin accepted a couple of sausages in bread and began to devour them, much to the delight of his new friends.

I was gobsmacked. They saw me looking at them and some of them waved, grinning widely as they sipped on beer and ate sausages in bread with tomato sauce. As I passed the jet boats I noticed tucked against the riverbank beside them was a huge red sea-kayak. I was tempted to pull in beside it but once again I knew I must continue. Such was my fate.

I carried on but now I was feeling worse than ever. I couldn't get the idea of 'real' food out of my head. I began to fantasise about it. First I wanted chicken. I wanted a chicken sandwich with buttered white bread and chilli sauce. In fact, what I needed was big hunks of crispy chicken. Yes, fried chicken pieces. I could almost taste them. Five minutes after that I wanted steak and chips and five minutes after that I wanted fish and chips. And five minutes later I wanted anything I could get my hands on. Hell, I'd have eaten multigrain, polyunsaturated, lentil, sesame seed-loaded, milk-biscuit sandwiches bathed in great dollops of peanut butter (I hate peanut butter) if I'd been offered them. I wasn't fussy.

As I paddled on, I realised I wasn't hungry: I was starving. I looked in my lifejacket pouches. There was nothing. I was surprised and annoyed at the same time. How could I have been so stupid? I tried to remember what had happened when I was preparing the night before. Graham had helped me get all my gear together for the kayak section and I was sure we had included more food than the nuts and the food bar I had half-eaten before it became a soggy mess. But that was gone now too. I had thrown it away and all I had to show for it was the sticky empty wrapper. I longed to have it back.

And what about all those bananas and bars I had seen floating in the water? A few competitors had taped food to the deck of their boat for easy access but clearly not all had chosen the right kind of tape. Now I longed to see a banana float by.

I began to blame Graham. He must have forgotten to put the food in. How could he let this happen? But was it really his fault? It was my race. I should have checked. I got angry with myself. I probably should have given myself a slap or two for being so stupid but I didn't have the energy for it.

I was now worried. No food meant no energy and no energy meant I might not have the strength to finish. How could I have been so stupid? I knew I was in trouble. I needed food so desperately I decided to ask another competitor for some.

I slowed up a little to wait for people to come by. The first chap to pass was flying. He paddled very quickly with great purpose and an excellent technique. I managed a half grin but he hardly saw me. He was never going to stop anyway. I let him go.

The next chap was the one. He was older, perhaps in his 50s, and seemed to have a pleasant grin etched permanently on his face. He came slowly up behind me and pulled up alongside. He seemed in no hurry. I didn't want to mess around so without even saying hello I said: 'Look I don't mean to be rude or anything but I don't seem to have packed enough food and I'm really suffering. Have you got anything you could spare?'

He laughed. It was not the response I was hoping for. I looked at him quizzically. 'What?'

He now had a huge grin on his face. 'Are you serious?' he asked.

'Absolutely,' I replied, starting to feel annoyed.

He chuckled again to himself and stopped paddling. 'You've got a large bag of food tucked into the net pocket at the back of your lifejacket.'

'You're joking?' I exclaimed and joined him in his laughter.

Three minutes later we were away again. His name was Dave. He helped hold my boat steady while I reached behind and grabbed the food bag and emptied its contents into the more accessible front pockets of my jacket. I stuffed as many pieces of apricot food bar into my mouth as I could manage and we carried on paddling. In no time the food began to have an effect. I felt stronger and a tad more optimistic. It was also great to have company.

Dave was an interesting bloke, and listening to him talking while I stuffed food into my mouth helped keep my mind off how uncomfortable I was feeling. It turned out he had done the race each of the last few years and really enjoyed it. He did it for the challenge and to have a fitness goal to aim for each year. His support crew was his wife, one of his sons and a couple of mates who had made the race a bit of a holiday together each year. He did other races too but the Coast to Coast had become a bit of a pilgrimage.

Dave chatted away and I listened while I looked around at the scenery. The terrain around the river was changing. The hills and cliffs that once towered over the water now began to recede and I felt we were coming out of the gorge. I pointed this out to Dave who said he thought Woodstock was around the next corner or so. A few minutes later and we were there.

Woodstock was a bit of a disappointment: it was the area where a dirt road came down off a series of small, scrub-covered plateaus to meet a large gravel flat beside the river. On the gravel were about 30 parked cars, empty jet-boat trailers, a smattering of spectators and a few officials. That was it. The name seemed grossly misleading. There was certainly no stock of wood anywhere to be seen. I don't know how featureless gravel flats get names like Woodstock.

Some of the officials sitting in deckchairs (on the edge of the featureless gravel flat known as Woodstock) looked up as we passed by. One of them yelled at us for our race numbers. We yelled them back. Dave told me they would radio ahead and write our numbers on a board so our support crews knew we were getting close. I could see the sense in that. Way ahead in the distance I could just make out some huge power pylons. I fixated on them and paddled on.

There was nothing to do now except work toward the finish. I had lost interest in conversation. There was no consolation in it any more and Dave had slowly drifted back behind me. Each time I turned around he was further back and after a while I stopped looking.

The river was easy to navigate: I followed the main braid wherever it went and there were few other options anyway. Other kayakers were stretched out ahead but none seemed to be paddling together. This was a section each person seemed destined to do alone. Alone in their misery. Nothing could relieve us – not food, nor companions. Nothing at all except the finish.

The wind came up. It blew in gusts, picking up dust and swirling it around and around like a mini-twister before another blast hit from a different angle, scattering the dust everywhere. Seagulls far from the sea walked around on the gravel picking at this and that while others sat in small groups and still others glided about aimlessly above.

It was around lunchtime but seemed much later. The sky was a glaring bright white with high cloud covering it as far as the eye could see. The cloud cover barely dimmed the sun and I was grateful again for the little protection the peak on my helmet afforded my eyes.

I struggled on. I felt weathered. The wind picked up as I neared the pylons. It whipped about my face. I peed when I needed to. I never stopped paddling. No one came past.

Finally I picked my way between some willow trees and the hills closed in again. The yellow dirt cliffs formed a short gorge. I knew what was coming. I rounded a corner and finally saw the gorge bridge up ahead, towering over the water. It sat majestically suspended between the cliffs on either side of the river.

I felt relief, although at the same time I knew it wasn't over yet: the river had one last trick up its sleeve. Ahead, I could see that the final bend was a seething, twisting cauldron of moving water. Beyond this cauldron, waiting on the stones of the river bank, I could also see hundreds of people watching and waiting. I knew I had to be careful. I certainly didn't want to fall out just short of my moment of glory and under the gaze of so many onlookers. Others had. On the bank was a very embarrassed-looking woman emptying out her boat with the aid of two male spectators.

I paddled the corner cautiously, wobbling a little as I did so, but when the swirling of the river subsided and the currents released their grip I powered under the bridge and turned towards the shore. The excitement of the occasion suddenly took hold of me. I had made it. 67 kilometres. Wow! I completely forgot my aches and pains as I charged the last few metres to where Graham, Chris and Tony had positioned themselves at the water's edge. I took a final few strokes, leant backwards to lift the bow, and slid up onto the stones, gliding to a halt.

Another milestone completed. Only 70 kilometres to go!

Chapter 20

The Last Ride

The second my boat came to a halt the lads leapt into action. Mine was the only boat to arrive for about a minute, so all eyes were on us. I hadn't noticed the lads' stern faces and the glazed look in their eyes, so I was rather surprised when I was ripped out of my kayak as if I was in first place. After an afternoon of watching other crews, the lads had obviously adopted a new, more professional transition technique. It seemed they had decided that seconds might be the difference between winning and losing. Apart from losing some skin on each shin, I thought the technique worked well. I was immediately ready to move.

The only problem was my legs. After nearly six hours cramped in the kayak they had ceased to operate as anything more than ballast. Seeing me in a crumbling heap before them did not deter the lads. Apparently they had seen this sort of thing before and in no time I was hauled back upright and was being frog-marched through the finish chute and up the dirt road to the bike transition area. Although I was the one doing the race I was pretty sure the applause and encouragement we received was for the lads and the sterling job they were doing to keep me moving, rather than any athletic endeavours on my part.

Halfway up the road the effort became too much for the lads and, thankfully, we all slowed to a walk. I began to shed pieces of kayaking equipment under the guise of a quick transition, but mostly because they were so darn heavy. I had wriggled out of my helmet, lifejacket and spray skirt by the time we reached the small plateau above the river where hundreds of bicycles were waiting in the midday heat. A loud bang told us someone had pumped up a bike tyre too high. We heard two more before we reached my own bike. When tyres are pumped to 120 pounds per square inch and left in direct sunlight it doesn't take long for them to

After an afternoon watching other crews at work, the lads rip me out of the kayak as though I was in first place. Hours cramped up in the boat have left my legs barely able to take my weight. Paul's Camera Shop

explode. One of the lads had thoughtfully laid a blanket over my bike to protect the tyres from the sun.

I slowly began to get into a new set of gear for the ride to the finish. At the same time I attempted to shove as much food as possible into my mouth. I was going to need the energy. As I struggled to eat and clothe myself Chris told me of the drama they'd had getting my bike fixed in time for my arrival. Apparently the morning's crash had buckled the back wheel and bent and twisted various other parts. Graham had made it his personal mission to get the bike back into running order. To do this he had badgered the race cycle mechanics mercilessly from the moment he discovered the bike had a problem until it was all straightened out.

'Thanthks, mayt,' I mumbled through a mouthful of food.

'I don't think I'm that popular around here at the moment,' he said, grinning happily.

Tony appeared beside us and said it would have been nice if he had been given some advance warning that my kayak was full of urine before he'd slung it over his shoulder. I could see his point and apologised.

Soon I was ready to go. Graham pushed the bike over to the road while I walked alongside, putting on my cycle helmet and gloves. We reached the road and I got on. I had no idea how I was going to summon enough energy to get to the finish but decided to give it my best shot. With an exuberant push that nearly threw me off the bike I was launched into the final leg.

After a few strokes of the pedals I was amazed. My legs felt fantastic! It was as if they had been reborn to cycling – not what I had expected after nearly six hours crammed in a kayak.

I powered up each of the three small hills between the terraces that lead out of the river valley and on to the Canterbury plains. The wind that was whipping about all over the place in the river valley for the last hour of the kayak leg seemed to be coming quite solidly from behind me. I felt as if I was flying. I looked down at my speedo and realised I virtually was. I was going 38 kilometres per hour. I couldn't remember ever having done that speed before on my own. I kept my head as low over the handlebars as my back could cope with and rode with great gusto. After about five minutes or so, when I realised I couldn't possibly keep this pace up all the way to town, I eased up and took a look behind. There was no one to be seen. I was a little surprised. There had been a number of others about at the transition point yet it seemed I had beaten them all to get on the bike and get going by a number of minutes! I wondered briefly if I had taken the wrong road but I couldn't recall having seen any side roads at all since leaving the river.

I cycled on but with a little less confidence than I had started with. Despite the fact that I had been in a bunch crash earlier in the morning I decided that ideally it would be good to ride to town with other cyclists. With a few of us taking turns at the front the journey would be a lot quicker and definitely more pleasant. I would just have to be careful to make sure I was ready for anything. I had no desire to be involved in another crash.

I looked up the road, straining through the heat haze for any sign of another rider in front but there was none. I had another quick look behind and saw a solitary figure had appeared in the distance. I thought that while it might take them a while to catch me it was good to know there would be other riders to work with should I need them.

I turned back just in time to see a race marshal suddenly appear in front of me waving wildly and directing me to take a side road. I quickly turned the handlebars to round the bend but with my weight so high I almost didn't make the turn. With my heart in my mouth I shot right over into the side of the road, narrowly avoiding the loose gravel and what would have been a highly embarrassing and completely unnecessary crash. I swore at my stupidity and determined to be more careful.

After the change of direction I noticed that the wind was now coming over my right shoulder rather than from directly behind. As a consequence my speed dropped to a more recognisable 32 kilometres per hour. I was a trifle disappointed but at least I wasn't facing a headwind. I momentarily imagined myself low on the bike and grimacing as I struggled into a howling gale at 20 kilometres per hour.

A bit further up the road I looked back again for the cyclist following and was surprised to see he had covered half the distance to me already. A few minutes later he had halved that gap and the next time I looked he was only a few metres back and preparing to pass. I was gobsmacked. Was I really that slow? I sat up to await his pass and see who he was.

He was a big, powerful-looking man, probably in his late 20s or early

Back on the bike and climbing out of the river valley. Only seventy kilometres to go! Paul's Camera Shop

30s. He saw me glancing at him and almost imperceptibly raised his eyebrows and gave the subtlest nod I had witnessed in my short cycling career. Clearly this guy was a class act.

As he passed I was surprised to see another rider was tucked in behind him. The second guy was a young man in his late teens or early 20s with reddish hair and a really flash bike. He grinned at me and, looking very pleased with himself, said something like 'jump on' as they swept on by. They were going so much faster than me that I had to do a little sprint just to latch on. I settled in behind, trying to keep up, my legs pumping like pistons. This guy was quick. I fumbled with my gears as I tried to change up. I finally found a suitable gear and started pushing hard to bridge the small gap that had begun to develop between me and the other two. We powered on with no let-up from the bloke out in front. I checked the speedo a number of times over the next few minutes. His speed remained consistently around the 43 kilometres per hour mark. This guy wasn't human. He was a machine.

The redheaded kid and I hung on for dear life in his wake as he charged toward Sumner. After a few more minutes of high speed we made one final left-hand turn on to the Old West Coast Road. This long straight road would take us to the edge of the city. It stretched off into the distance before us, the broken white line fading into the heat haze.

Keeping a close eye on the rear wheel of the kid in front of me, I backed off a metre or so and stole a cautious sip of water from my bottle. I had begun to notice signs of the odd loss in concentration: a sudden little swerve here, a wobble there. He looked uncomfortable on the bike and had begun changing positions on his seat every half a minute or so. First he would sit very low, crouching just above the handlebars, presenting a perfect profile to the wind, before sitting up suddenly and wobbling about. After peering out on the left past the big bloke in front he would come back into position, wriggle on his seat and settle back into the low crouched position again.

When he moved to take a drink from his bottle I quickly backed off again. His erratic behaviour soon became a real concern and I started to wonder whether I might need to say something, when suddenly he was on the move again. With his head down low over the handlebars and his eyes seemingly transfixed on the road below his front wheel, the kid began to veer slowly off to the left, toward the grass verge and the fence just beyond it. At first I thought he was drifting to the side of the other cyclist to see past him up the road, but he didn't stop.

Just as I opened my mouth to shout a warning he suddenly looked up and violently swung back into line. I saw him coming and took evasive action. As I did so I looked down at the rough-chip road surface whizzing by beneath my wheels and thought how very painful a crash would be. While the kid's near-miss seemed to have woken him up and improved his concentration, it was too late for me. There was no way I wanted to be anywhere near this lunatic, least of all behind him.

The 'machine' riding in front obviously wasn't going to risk having his back wheel smashed out from under him, so when I got up off my seat to surge past the kid the 'machine' accelerated as well. In no time we had left him far behind. I looked back a while later to see him well in the distance and sitting up high on his bike. He was making no attempt to keep low into the wind and was all over the road. I wasn't unhappy to see him go.

Back with the 'machine' the pace showed no sign of letting up. We roared along the road with him doing all the work at the front and me hanging on as best I could. I felt a wee bit guilty benefiting from all his hard work but he didn't say anything so I figured I might as well enjoy it. No sooner had I absolved myself of any guilt associated with a free ride than he quite suddenly pulled out to the left and looked back at me as if to say, 'Well come on, lazy boy, are you going to have a turn or not?'

I was no keener to take the lead than I was to ride straight into a tree but felt I had to. The unwritten rules of cycling are acknowledged everywhere and anyone seeking the benefits of riding with companions had two choices: obey or be cut loose. I chose to obey.

I took the lead to do my share and was immediately stunned by the power of the wind. I got as low as I could and pedalled with vigour. I wanted to show Mr Machine that I was a worthy companion and one worth keeping. If he got a bit of a rest behind me and felt I was contributing, then as the stronger cyclist he might just decide to stay with me. This way I would have a much quicker ride to the finish. It was a long shot but I clung to the hope he would show mercy. I needn't have bothered. Whereas before my turn in the lead we had been going at a steady 40 kilometres per hour, within seconds of my arrival at the sharp end of our bunch of two our speed began to decline. I did somehow manage 34 kilometres per hour for about 30 seconds but 30 seconds after that I was down to 31 kilometres per hour. I struggled on for a bit longer and then pulled off to the side. Without a word he just blew on by and kept going. There was no way I could catch his back wheel so I just watched him go. I felt a little annoyed but could hardly blame him. He was a hell of a cyclist and I was probably no better than his grandmother. Still, I was sorry to see him go. Now I would have to face the road alone.

I rode on, watching him disappear at a great rate of knots. I thought how truly wonderful it would be to be a good cyclist. No need to rely on feeble cyclists but able to ride alone and still maintain a good speed. I guess all average athletes like to dream. Today this was mine.

My thoughts soon returned to the task at hand. I figured I had only been riding for about 20 minutes. By my calculations I still had a couple of hours to go, and possibly on my own. The thought was too depressing to contemplate.

Not only that, but now that I was riding at a much more sedate speed I noticed that the wind had, as I feared it would, swung around from a tail wind to almost directly in front of me. I groaned in disappointment. The outlook was not getting any better. I wondered if there was any prospect of joining other cyclists coming up the road.

I took a look behind. Way off in the distance I could see a solitary figure weaving about the road. I looked again a few minutes later. The figure was no closer. I could rule out help from behind, at least in the short term.

It was just me versus the wind.

Normally when cycling I sit quite upright with a straight back and my hands resting on the highest point on the handlebars. While this position is quite comfortable it is about as aerodynamic as the side of a building. I decided I needed to change my profile into something sleeker. Considering what I had to work with, I wasn't too hopeful of pulling it off. I decided to prepare for a battle, a battle against the wind.

For a start I ducked down as low as I could, with my head just above the handlebar stem and my hands down on the handlebar drops. I didn't feel comfortable at all. My seat was considerably higher than the lowest part of the handlebars and so to reach them I was forced to bend in a most unnatural way. I felt so strained I imagined the slightest twist would see a disc explode out of my back. Despite the discomfort I was lower. I took a quick look at the speedo. There it was in black and white: an improvement of one kilometre per hour.

However, my new aerodynamic position meant my stomach was squashed into my chest while my knees pumped violently up and down only a few inches from my chin. I could see the potential for a nasty accident. A small error in judgement might see the equivalent of a perfectly executed uppercut send me to never-never land. I imagined waking up in the grass at the side of the road with a thumping headache, a broken jaw and wondering what the hell had happened.

I had other problems. Keeping a weather eye on my knees, I moved around a little and discovered the most comfortable position for my head had me looking through the front wheel spokes at the ground. Of course, at some stage I was going to need to see where I was going and would have to lift my head up. While I wanted to stay in my low position I realised I needed some kind of compromise. I decided a quick glance up at where I was going every 10 seconds or so was enough to protect my neck as well as keep me on track and out of the grass verge at the side of the road. But only just. A couple of times over the next 20 minutes I would look up just in time to catch myself veering off to either the middle of the road or the verge when I had been convinced I was travelling in a straight line.

Competition can lead people to do things they ordinarily wouldn't. It dawned on me that I was no exception. Here I was hunched over my bike like a professional, low and mean, at one with the machine. In all my training I had never ridden my bike like this. As I had cruised around the countryside on training rides I generally sat bolt-upright and as comfortable as possible. If there was a headwind I just went slower. It never occurred to me that it might be a good idea to position myself as low as possible.

But now something in me had changed. I had become competitive. I wanted to go faster. Not only was I putting up with significant discomfort for the sake of speed but I was, in a perverse sort of way, enjoying it. It was a challenge. It was a private battle. There was no one to watch me, no one to impress. It was just me versus the wind.

I had learnt something new about myself: I could cope with the suffering. If I really wanted to I could turn it off by simply sitting up. But I didn't want to. I wanted to ride, at least for a while, like a real cyclist. I didn't want to give in. I didn't want to capitulate to comfort. I wanted another reason to be proud of myself. I had already surprised myself a number of times over the last two days and I wanted more. So I kept going. After a while I think I even began to adapt a little to my new position on the bike. I think for a while I almost felt comfortable, in an uncomfortable sort of way. I began to get into a good rhythm. I focused on the ground just ahead of the front wheel and pedalled on and on. It was stirring stuff. I was almost disappointed when a few minutes later I was surprised by the arrival of a bunch of eight cyclists.

They whizzed up beside me and were past in a second. I had to get up and pedal hard just to get onto the back wheel of the last in line, but once there it was nice to sit up and have a rest. The group worked well together. One by one they took turns of little more than 30 seconds at the front before pulling off to the side. As they faded past me on their way to the back of the line I was able to have a look at each in turn.

First to drop back was a tall, wiry chap with a gaunt face and a pair of very geeky glasses. As he came past he nodded at me and said 'Gidday, we're trying to keep the speed around 35, 36, but do what you can.' I nodded back. I took a quick drink and a few deep breaths. I still felt quite tired from the effort of cycling by myself and wondered if I was up to the task.

The next person to fade back past me after a good solid turn at the front was a woman. She wasn't a big woman and she rode what looked almost like a child-size bike but looked like a strong cyclist. She had big, powerful thighs and hunched low over the bike like a pro. She grinned as she passed and with a 'Hi' she dropped back behind the tall skinny guy. It was such a friendly group I felt like I was cycling with the Waltons.

Suddenly I noticed the speed had picked up. At the same time there was a lot more talk coming from someone at the front of the bunch. I couldn't pick up what was being said but it sounded like encouragement. The pace never slackened and I started to find it difficult. Soon I was working hard just to keep my place behind the next rider. Some of the others seemed to be finding it difficult too. The chap in front of me was breathing heavily and someone behind me swore something about 'the bloody idiot' up front. A quick glance at the speedo confirmed it. We were now doing 40 kilometres per hour.

The speed stayed the same for about two minutes before easing off just as suddenly as it started. Moments later another tall, skinny chap began to fade toward the rear of the group. This guy was all business. He had a greeny-brown carbon-fibre bike that looked as if it had been taken straight off the set of a Star Trek movie. Its sleek lines and smooth surfaces seemed to have been made with one purpose in mind: to cheat the wind. The rider matched his machine. His helmet was like the nose cone of an aeroplane with a window at the front. Instead of finishing abruptly at the back of his head like most of the helmets I'd seen, his extended out about a foot beyond his head. He was decked out in what looked like superior gear – a very sharp and expensive-looking US Postal cycling team uniform – and his body appeared to be completely hairless, he didn't even have hair on his arms. Everything about him looked smooth and sleek. There was nothing for the wind to grab onto.

As he slowly drifted back into line I made eye contact with him and nodded. He completely ignored me and turned to look back up the road. I gave him the benefit of the doubt. Maybe he hadn't seen me. After all, I was over a metre away! I shrugged and carried on.

The pace was now a lot more to my liking and I understood why when the next guy drifted back. He was a thick-set chap with an infectious smile. He rode as if he didn't have a care in the world and joked and laughed with everyone as he cruised down the line to the back of the group. Everyone, that is, except the serious guy with the expensive bike.

The group worked together well for the next few kilometres; everyone except for the serious chap on the flash bike. Instead of taking a 30-second turn at the front on around 35 kilometres an hour he blasted out 40 or more kilometres an hour for two minutes at a time. This was not appreciated. We weren't good enough to appreciate it. At the end of his turn we would all be gasping for breath and trying to recover before our own turn at the front. One of the other riders asked him to ease up but to no avail. His next two turns at the front were just as fast.

The funny guy had had enough, and as we zipped along the road he began to tease him with a continual stream of annoying banter. He dubbed him 'Lance'. It was beautiful to listen to.

'So, Lance, that was a great effort last go, you had us hanging on for dear life.'

'My name's not Lance.'

'Forty ks! Yep, you were smoking. Say, Lance, that's an amazing bike, is that Shimano gear?'

'Yes, but I'm not called Lance.'

The funny guy ignored him and carried on. 'Well, I think Shimano make excellent gear, don't you?'

Lance just couldn't get away from him.

Next time it was his turn at the front I could clearly hear the funny guy teasing him.

'Oh, you're doing great, Lance, keep it up, Lance, spank it, Lance.'

Lance did his two minutes at 40 kilometres and came past on his way back. Since his effort nearly killed us we let him have it: 'Nice work, Lance.' 'Top stuff, Lance.'

The funny guy came down the line after his turn grinning from ear to ear. We all smiled back with the exception of Lance. He was getting pissed off. On his next turn at the front Lance just rode off and left us. The funny guy yelled after him as he disappeared up the rode. 'Dig it in, Lance, it's your tour.' We all burst into laughter. Lance didn't turn round. He had a tour to win.

Life without Lance was a lot more bearable. We still rode fast but at a much more manageable speed for a group of our ability. We ticked along taking 30-second turns at the front and keeping close to around 35 kilometres per hour for what seemed like an age. We kept in close formation, communicated well and changed leader seamlessly. Encouraging banter flowed back and forth and each time a member did their turn at the front the group would acknowledge the effort. It was magic stuff. It struck me that despite the fact that this was very much a race of individuals, here we were working together as an incredibly efficient unit to achieve our common goal. Not only that, it was great fun to be part of. Struggling alone along an endless straight road with next to nothing to look at but empty paddocks, long macrocarpa hedges and a farmer's letterbox every half a kilometre had nothing on this. We were belting along the road oblivious to all but the hum of the bikes, the few inches between each wheel and the rate of our breathing. It took all my concentration, but I was really enjoying being part of such a cohesive group. Judging by the smiles it seemed the others were having an equally good time. It was a high point in the race for me.

But all good things must come to an end and for the second time on this ride I was completely taken by surprise as a much bigger bunch reared up out of nowhere. They cruised up beside us in two long lines, the hiss of the bikes making them sound like two giant snakes. We tagged on near the rear of one of the lines and stayed together for a while but the new bunch was less focused and ceased to operate as efficiently. It revolved within itself constantly, changing function and form and in no time we were split up and swallowed.

I found myself behind a cyclist whose manner seemed familiar. He shifted about awkwardly on his bike and from time to time wobbled out of position, causing a minor scare as those around him took evasive action. It was the young redheaded kid from earlier. I groaned. Of all the cyclists to end up behind I had to end up behind the baby-faced assassin. It was only a matter of time before he made a serious mistake and brought everyone behind him down in a screaming heap. I decided not to be his first victim. As soon as a space cleared beside me I got out from behind him and crossed over into the other line of cyclists. One of the other cyclists recognised what I was doing and gave a knowing smirk.

Over the next few minutes the redheaded kid betrayed himself by weaving about regularly. He was an accident waiting to happen. One by one the cyclists behind him began to notice and with a few whispers and gestures they silently cleared out from behind his back wheel and into the other line. No one wanted to risk a crash. It was understandable. You might lose some teeth, break your wrist, collarbone or maybe your arm. You might get a head injury and be off work for weeks. And all this just because some keen kid hadn't taken the time to practise riding as a member of a bunch.

The funny guy must have noticed him as well. It didn't take him long to home in. He pulled up beside the lad. 'Hey, Lance, how's it going?' His opening made me smile.

The kid ignored him.

'Come on, Lance, you can talk to me.'

The kid suddenly realised the funny guy was actually talking to him.

'Oh, I'm not Lance,' he replied.

The funny guy ignored his answer and carried on. 'Nice gloves, Lance, they look as if they'd be useful if you fell off.'

The kid just smiled awkwardly.

'Say, Lance, do you want to know how to find out if other people think you're a safe rider?'

The kid looked at him quizzically. He wasn't sure what was going on.

The funny guy asked again. 'Well, do ya?'

'What?'

'Want to know how to find out if people think you're a safe rider.'

'I don't know... I guess so.'

The funny guy leant toward him as if to impart a deadly secret.

'You look behind you.'

The kid thought about it for a while then slowly took a peek behind. All the other riders were strung out in a long line beside him. There was no one behind him at all.

As he scanned the faces down our line he noticed that everyone who had heard the conversation was looking at him. You could almost see the moment it dawned on him that no one was riding behind him because he was dangerous. I almost felt sorry for him as his face dropped and he turned back. He was embarrassed. The funny guy never said another word to him and over the next few minutes as the bunch revolved around itself the young redhead quietly slipped to the very back of the line. I didn't notice him again.

As the bunch powered on we were passing more and more letterboxes. I assumed this could only mean one thing – we were approaching the outskirts of the city.

Two minutes later we swung around a bend and on to the main road. Quite suddenly the pace was on. It was as if someone at the front of the bunch had seen the finish line and decided to make a bolt for it. Like all those around me I was suddenly faced with the choice of either getting up off my barely comfortable bike seat and pedalling like a lunatic or being left behind to struggle to the finish on my own. I decided that if at all possible I should try to stick with the bunch. I wound up my tired legs as fast as I could and, making sure to stay right in the slipstream of the rider in front of me, I gave it all I could. The bunch was going so fast

I knew it would be impossible for us to sustain such an effort. I looked at the speedo. 38, 39, 40, 41. What the hell was going on up there? 42, 43.

In no time my already tired body was truly suffering. My heart was pounding in my chest and my legs were screaming for oxygen, but I couldn't stop. I needed this bunch. With all the willpower I possessed I ordered my body to keep going and held on for all I was worth. Finally, just as suddenly as it began, the pace slowed – and not a moment too soon. My legs had just begun to quiver weakly, and had lost some co-ordination. It was as if they were on the verge of some kind of meltdown. I sucked in the air like a drowning swimmer and slowly began to recover.

The pace of the bunch was still relatively high and while I didn't yet feel completely recovered from the big surge I did find the current pace manageable. Most importantly I had survived. I was still a part of the bunch.

Others were not so lucky. I looked back to see four or five stragglers strung out behind us, hunched over their handlebars looking sad and defeated as they struggled on alone into the wind. Their pain and discomfort would last just a little bit longer than for the rest of us.

We soon left the stragglers far behind. I joined those around me at the back of the bunch in speculation about why the pace had suddenly come on and then off. A quick zip out to the side of the bunch and a brief look up the road gave us an idea. We decided that after the excitement of coming onto the main road the leaders had flown along until reaching a small bend. They had charged around it expectantly, only to see another long stretch of road leading into the distance. When they realised the edge of the suburbs was still a bit further on the pace had relaxed. We decided it was as good a theory as any and to be wary of when we actually did hit the suburbs.

When I mentioned I thought it was crazy to be pushing so hard now, considering we still had to travel 25 kilometres across the city to the coast, there were gasps of surprise. I realised I was surrounded by people from out of town.

'I thought we were nearly there,' said a man around my age, looking dejected.

'It's not that far is it?' said another, equally dejectedly.

'Bugger,' said someone else.

The pace began to rise again. I took a look up ahead and saw a round-about and a service station about 300 metres ahead. It was the edge of the suburbs. Now I was in trouble: the pace would come on again.

A movement in the distance caught my eye. There were people standing at the side of the road. They had to be spectators. In the last hour we had begun to see small groups of spectators along the road as we whizzed past. Some had deck chairs and blankets and were having picnics. They cheered and shouted encouragement, yelled this and that or just waved. One held up a sign exhorting someone called 'Lazy Doug' to greater things. At one stage our bunch was stunned into silence after passing a group of three elderly ladies sitting regally attired in hats and dresses on little cane chairs. They clapped politely as our colourful circus hissed by.

Ordinarily I would welcome spectators. Like anybody I thrive on encouragement. That anyone would come out to watch an event where someone of my athletic pedigree might be competing was cause for celebration. But right now I feared them and wished they'd stayed home. Spectators meant trouble.

Why? I knew that as soon as the boys at the front of the bunch noticed there was an audience up ahead they would be powerless to resist the chance to impress and the pace would go crazy again. The last thing I needed was another violent acceleration. Almost as soon as I had thought it, it happened.

The pace picked up alright but this time it went ballistic. By the time we reached the roundabout my legs were beyond tired. Once again they screamed at me to stop and rest as they quivered on the verge of breakdown and I waited for them to simply collapse and crumble off the pedals. They didn't. Somehow I kept going, and going, and going. It was strangely unreal. I was hanging on way past the point where I thought I could. Others were falling off the back of the bunch, which was now down to about 15 from the 25 or so we started with. I didn't know how I was surviving, but I was, and that was all that mattered.

The bunch was beginning to lose its form and began revolving in a way I had not seen before. It seemed to form two small ovals. The one at the rear was fairly stable but the one at the front kept revolving first one way and then the next as different cyclists took the lead. The lead was changed so frequently and in such a haphazard way there was no telling who would lead and when. I found myself at the rear of this oval and then quite suddenly at the front. A moment later one side of the oval detached and swept past me on the left. At the same time the rest of the cyclists behind me swept past on the right. I whipped in behind those passing on the right. As I hung on grimly behind the riders in front I noticed there was no one directly behind me. A small gap of a few metres had opened up. Over the next minute or so I took glimpses behind as the leading cyclists inched back and with a huge effort they finally closed the gap. It was very exciting.

We were in the suburbs proper now. There were houses on both sides of the road, spectators milling about in groups or sitting at the roadside. The roads were not closed to the general public so there were cars everywhere. Car horns tooted from all directions. The road was wide and some cars even came alongside as passengers shouted encouragement from the windows. It was a carnival atmosphere. Everybody knew it was Coast to Coast day.

Our bunch charged on towards our first set of traffic lights. A policeman held up the other streams of traffic and beckoned us through. It was a great feeling. We swept around the bend, barely missing a beat, and charged off on our new heading. We whizzed through another set of lights and onwards. The bunch was clearly excited now. The long hard slog of the open road was over. We were now well within the confines of the city. This was the world we knew. This was the environment in which we worked, lived and trained. The roads were smooth and inviting and the usually threatening traffic had been thwarted. For a brief moment the mighty, relentless machine of the city stopped as we swept by. This was our moment, our time.

We pushed on through to the next intersection. Men in uniform appeared and the traffic parted like the Red Sea. They held up the walls with raised arms as we raced on by to the start of a short motorway. Then with a flick of the wrist they released the tide behind us.

We charged up the lower slope of an overpass and I knew I was finished. My legs were spent. It was over. The bunch slowly eased away and I couldn't respond. I watched them go. Another rider dropped off and then another and then they were gone. I carried on alone up to the top of the overpass. There was a good view from the top. Christchurch is such a flat city you don't need to get very high to be able to see for miles in every direction. I surveyed the surrounding hills and marvelled at the extent of the greenery that seemed to encompass much of the city. For a few moments I forgot about the race and took in the view.

As I began to descend down the other side I was surprised at how far my bunch had gotten away from me. The other two riders who dropped shortly after me had formed their own bunch of two and were also disappearing up the road ahead of me.

I resigned myself to a lonely slog through the city. But first I had to get along the short motorway. It ran for a few kilometres around the back of factories and other businesses. My speed since the departure of the bunch had dropped back to a much less respectable 28 kilometres per hour but it felt slower. Cars were whizzing by at nearly four times that speed and I felt as if I was standing still.

I also felt a lot more vulnerable. Some of the cars seemed to come awfully close as they whipped past. It was nerve-wracking and it was with some relief that I finally crested a rise and began a short descent to the end of the motorway and back into suburbia.

Although in the suburbs I was partially protected from its effects, I noticed the headwind was picking up the closer I got to the coast. I got lower on the handlebars but was still unable to stop my speed from dropping. It continued to do so over the next few minutes and eventually settled at around 24 kilometres per hour. After the excitement and thrill of riding at speed with a bunch, grovelling along alone at a very slow 24 kilometres per hour was a humbling experience. It got worse.

I rode on toward a series of intersections, desperately fighting the wind and struggling to keep forward momentum. When I was about a hundred metres from the first one I glanced up and saw that the policeman in control was preparing to halt the traffic. He must have seen a few groups fly through at high speed and so not wanting to get caught napping he dutifully stepped out in to the middle of the road in plenty of time.

Then he waited.

And waited. And waited.

The people in their cars waited too.

I could see them up ahead peering down the road as they tried to work out what on earth the hold-up was. Even the policeman began to look bemused. I felt like a tortoise. With all these people staring intently at me I finally made it to the intersection. I looked about in embarrassment. Apart from the quiet hum of all the waiting cars there was complete silence.

Here were all these people (there was at least 20 cars) waiting for some great Coast to Coast athlete to charge through like a bolt of lightning as he threw everything into one last effort for glory. Instead some chubby little bloke on a clapped-out old bike struggled past looking as though he had half-killed himself riding to the local store because he'd heard that pies were going cheap.

After that humiliation I made a much better fist of the next few intersections. Between intersections I slowed down, sat up, caught my breath, had a drink and generally saved my energy. When I approached the next one I switched back into business mode. I got down low, put on my game face and pedalled like a man possessed. Spectators and bystanders watched in awe as a serious-looking cyclist roared on through the intersection, eyes focused intensely on the road, his face set in steely determination. People clapped and cheered and some even tooted car horns. The cyclist did not look round. He was far too professional. He rode steadily off into the distance. At the next intersection he charged through again, impervious to the clapping and cheering. Cars pulled alongside with kids hanging out the windows and watching him in awe so he had no time to rest. Another intersection, more stopped traffic, stares and clapping. He drove on, an unrelenting cycling machine. This was what people had come to see. I certainly wasn't going to let them down.

Not long after I left the busy roads and intersections behind and rode through the back of another industrial area. I wilted. Frankly I was glad to be away from the gaze of the public. It was bloody hard work trying to be a Coast to Coast hero. My legs were spent, my backside ached and my neck was sore. I wanted to go home. I felt as if I had nothing left. Food and drink were no consolation and there was no one to ride with. The bunch in front had disappeared and only God knew what had happened to the rest of the racers behind me.

It was obvious I was going through another difficult patch and again I could not stop the flow of negative thoughts. All I wanted to do was get off my bike and never sit on it again. I fantasised about stopping.

'Right here, right now. Go on, just stop and get off the bike.'

But I didn't stop. I couldn't. I knew what I had to do. I knew once again that there was no way I would stop until I got to the end.

I began to think about finishing.

The finish. I was close now. I would just think about the finish. I would focus on that. That would help me through this.

I visualised running through a long chute across the sand towards a big banner saying 'Finish'. I imagined crowds of people cheering. I imagined the buzz of excitement and the sense of achievement I would feel. With these images in my head and a new-found sense of purpose masking any discomfort, I pushed on.

The route took a sharp right-hand turn at another police-controlled intersection and I charged around it with real conviction. I felt so much better it was unnerving. Ignoring everything except the patch of road immediately in front of my front wheel, I began to work harder and harder. I knew I was going faster but ignored my speedo. This was not about speed, this was about my body and what it could give. It would give what it could and that would be good enough. I wouldn't put a number on it.

All the time I thought of the finish. It would be great. I was going to make it. It had been difficult and yes, at times I had wanted to give up but I hadn't and now I was nearly there. I had worked hard to get my body ready and now, towards the end, I had found mental and physical strength I didn't know I had.

I would have crossed my country from one side to the other. I had touched the water on the west coast and soon I would touch it on the east coast. That would be a first. There were lots of others too. I had cycled in huge bunches, struggled on my own and even survived a crash. I had run over a mountain pass, kayaked a river for hours on end, pissed in my boat. And I had suffered.

If I could do all that then I could do anything. It was just a matter of persisting.

I crossed a small bridge and made my way toward the edge of the Christchurch estuary. The road cut across its southern edge and directly into the full force of the strong onshore breeze. A sea of angry whitecaps swept past on my left and smashed into the rocks beside the road.

I surveyed my path ahead.

Open road.

No cover.

Head-wind blowing like a bastard.

Good. Bring it on. It could have been a hurricane, I didn't care. I was going to get there – eventually. I wasn't going to stop.

I looked down at the road in front of my front wheel and pushed on.

I never even heard the bunch coming. Third one of the day. They just appeared out of nowhere and slowly fought their way past. They hardly seemed to be going any faster than I was but after the first five or six had passed they moved in front of me and I found myself in the middle. Pedalling suddenly became easier. I sheltered there all along the exposed causeway. At the end of it we moved back amongst the shelter of houses, trees, fences and suburbia. The pace increased but only marginally. These people were tired. I soon found myself near the front.

As I looked around, I came to the realisation that if I stayed where I was I was going to finish in the bunch. I was going to run across the sand and down the chute with everyone else, as part of the crowd, just another competitor.

This was not what I had imagined. It was not what I had dreamed of and it was not what I wanted. I decided to do something about it.

I took a sip of water, bit my lip till it hurt and then rode up to and off the front of the bunch. Come hell or high water, I decided, I was going to finish alone. It was just a case of whether it would be in front of the bunch or behind it.

I got out of my seat and pushed and pushed and pushed until my legs were screaming and then I pushed some more. I rode and I suffered. I put everything into maintaining the hardest pace I could possibly manage. After a minute and a half I looked back. I was well clear. Not only that, but I had blown apart the bunch. I assumed some of the others had gone out after me because there were riders strung out all over the place. I had broken away! Holy smoke! I couldn't believe it.

Now I was really excited. The realisation of what I had done spurred me on and even though I felt incredibly tired I went again as hard as I could for as long as I could. It hurt, but I pushed on through the pain.

There was no way I wanted to be caught this close to the finish.

When my thighs started to falter and I could push no longer I sat back on my seat and keeping as low as possible I took another look back. I was still well clear. I felt relieved. I would just have to hold on until the finish and hope I had done enough.

My focus shifted from my pain to the road ahead. I registered little else of my surroundings. A yacht club, some tethered boats, a big rock. I rode along beside the sea and turned the final corner. When I had gone a hundred metres past it I turned and took a look behind. There was no one there. I had done it. I rode the last few hundred metres to the finish chute, got off my bike and tried to run. I felt horribly stiff and sore but I crabbed my way onto the sand and into the empty chute.

As I felt the glare of hundreds of faces lining the chute a huge surge of energy pulsed through my body. I had done it, I was going to finish!

The announcer garbled something and the crowd cheered. As the significance of what I had achieved struck me I felt as if I glided the last few metres and under the banner. Robin Judkins appeared from somewhere, handed me a can of Speight's and shook my hand. It was over.

The best feeling in the world! Two cans of hard-earned Speight's from Robin Judkins, under the shadow of the finish line banner. Paul's Camera Shop

Epilogue

I have just been down to Sumner beach for the afternoon.

There is something going on there.

It is like a carnival. Hundreds of smiling faces, children running about, noise, colour and laughter. The sun is shining brightly and flags flap gently in the breeze.

It's Coast to Coast day.

Twelve months on and much about the Coast to Coast is the same. The athletes still roll in one by one or in groups, wide, satisfied grins and soaring spirits masking aching bodies and tired minds. Over the PA the announcer shouts out their names, occupations and 10-word resumé to the crowd who cheer every competitor their last few glorious metres. The emotion and fervour washes down the finish chute like waves on a beach, no two quite the same.

Robin Judkins is still there. He stands smiling under the finishing banner, presiding over his creation like a proud father. Quietly detached and lost in thought, he awaits the next finisher. Then the PA heralds the imminent arrival of another's journey's end and he changes. Like a contortionist, the clown of the carnival, he reads the state of each competitor the split second he sees them and he lives the last moments of their journey with these, his children. An emotional mirror, he aches with the aching, frowns with the frowning and he exults with the exultant. He stands, arms raised in triumph, to greet a similarly victorious finisher.

He understands. Years ago, when he'd first tested the course, he'd felt those same emotions. He knew he'd stumbled upon a winner. He bottled it and sold it and called it the Coast to Coast. Smart man. Now his name and face are synonymous with the race – impossible to separate. The ultimate finish-line accessory, he poses for photographs with each of them. His grin will adorn mantelpieces all over the country. Pride of place.

As the finisher and his entourage move away Judkins' smile lingers, then fades. He turns again to wait, quiet and alone. Like the parent of teenagers he'll be waiting until the last one comes home. As the PA calls out another name he slowly, tiredly rises from his seat and a smile begins to grow on his face.

Yes, much is still the same.

Competitors mill about excitedly with support crews, family and friends. There are hugs and back slaps and congratulations. Eager ears listen as stories are told. Comrades pass by. Hands shake and compliments flow. Mutual respect. We did it, the Coast to Coast!

Others limp about slowly. Frivolous vows are made – 'I'll never ever do that again' – only to be broken the next day. But the enthusiasm is contagious. It drifts through the crowd looking for eager hearts. One by one next year's racers are found. Some don't even know it yet. They watch silently, lost in thought, asking questions: Could I do this? What will it take?

Nothing has changed. The excitement is still palpable. It's like backstage at a charity rock concert. Acts come and go, sweaty, pumped and satisfied. I watch the faces, see the joy, and the pain and I feel good. I like this place, these people. I wonder if this experience will change them the way it changed me.

It started here at the beach: I went home exhausted, draped over friends and family. I did nothing for weeks. I ate a lot and sometimes I slept during the day. Slowly I began to feel normal again.

Then one day I came home from work, I put on my shoes and went for a run. Two days later I did it again. The following week I rode my bike to work. Soon I was doing something every day. What was normal for me had begun to change.

There were other changes: I felt more confident. I wanted to do better in life. I developed some goals. I worked harder at work, did more with my time. I wanted to become a better husband, a better father, a better person.

I have noticed I have less fear. I don't seem to have as much time for it. I have too many things to do.

On Sundays we started going for family walks. Small ones at first – the museum, the park. But later we went to the hills. Sweating and puffing our way up the tracks, stopping for water and sweets. Then on we'd trudge, puffing and sweating and working until we finally made the top. We took photos. There is something special about a view you've earned.

We got some gear. Hats for the cold, jackets for the wind, a small daypack with enough zips, straps and pockets to keep us busy for hours. Tools for a new lifestyle.

We started biking together. We bought a bike for one child and a device for towing the other. We began to explore the city. We found tracks and paths that led to all sorts of interesting places.

Spending more time together, we became closer. There will be other changes soon, new challenges. We are having another child. It seems appropriate. A new life for a new life.

Of course it's not all roses. But when courage fails and I wonder how I will ever cope with this or that, I like to look back and remember.

I remember long roads, harsh mountains, jagged rocks and cold rivers. I remember cramps and crashes, the discomfort and the exhaustion. I remember the pain and the suffering, I remember the struggle.

I remember it all.

And then I remind myself that I overcame it all. Each obstacle one by one, each part of the journey piece by piece.

I remind myself I once crossed my country from coast to coast.

I remember and I am proud.